LIGHTHOUSES

OF

HAMPTON ROADS

LIGHTHOUSES

OF

HAMPTON ROADS

A History

BENJAMIN H. TRASK

THE
History
PRESS

Published by The History Press
Charleston, SC
www.historypress.com

First published 2023

Manufactured in the United States

ISBN 9781467146159

Library of Congress Control Number: 2023932157

To Roy and Betty Giles, who share their expansive view of Hampton Roads with the world.

CONTENTS

PREFACE

A lighthouse evokes a vision of an isolated tower tended by an aged mariner. This seafarer, who, in their prime, roamed the oceans, now spends their autumn years smoking their pipe and watching the sunset. The lighthouses in southeastern Virginia did harbor these old salts, and most of the caretakers were white men from Virginia or North Carolina. Nevertheless, this is a narrow view of the region's keepers. The caretakers also included immigrants, women and formerly enslaved people. These diverse guardians of the lights diligently attended their respective stations and were often recognized for their lifesaving exploits. With that in mind, newspapers bestowed on the experienced keepers the honorific title of "captain."

Some of the keepers lived with their families at the light stations. However, most men worked at screwpile lighthouse stations, separated from loved ones. Their typical rotations were about twenty-two days on duty followed by eight days of leave. This arrangement allowed many "wickies" to commute from their respective homes. Especially noteworthy was the flow of personnel who came from two seafaring communities that became the "cradles of keepers" for the Fifth District. These two locales were Mathews County, Virginia, and the Outer Banks of North Carolina. The career pattern for these mariners can be found in a simple phrase: "follow the water." This course of employment was inked like a tattoo. These mariners served in every capacity in the lighthouse service: tenders, lightship skippers and crew members, lighthouse keepers and maintenance shop tradesmen.

This diversity among the keepers is just one fascinating aspect of lighthouse history in the greater Hampton Roads area. This monograph will explore the stories of eleven stations, their keepers and the interrelated events. These sentinels illuminated the waterways as warships, commercial vessels and fishing watercraft scudded along Hampton Roads, the Chesapeake Bay and the James River. The settings for these stations varied. Two of the installations were eventually surrounded by army posts. The image of the cozy confines of Old Point Comfort became a recurring feature for newspaper human interest articles. However, within sight of Old Point, the manmade island that was the Thimble Shoal Lighthouse was often struck by errant vessels. Likewise, just a few miles from Thimble Shoal, the lonely Back River station remained under constant threat from erosion.

Chronologically, the scope of this project extends from the mid-1700s to the present. Each lighthouse station's history has been arranged as a chapter. The lights are within the coast guard's Fifth District. Readers should keep in mind the history of the station in this study starts in earnest with the construction of a lighthouse, even though some stations began as lightships. Also, a station's structure may have changed from a screwpile to a caisson lighthouse, but still, the station is the same. Consequently, the old and new Cape Henry Lighthouses are just different beacons for the same station. Also, while the chapters on each lighthouse function independently, there is overlapping, relevant information in other chapters. So, please use the index to get a complete history of each light.

This book is arranged on the operation date of a fixed light tower, starting with Cape Henry (1792) and concluding with Newport News Middle Ground (1891). Generally, the chapters focus on the times when resident keepers tended the beacons. The Cape Henry Lighthouse was the first lighthouse built completely using federal funds. Navy chaplain Walter Colton called the old Cape Henry Lighthouse "a venerable, attached friend." The stations range from a tower boasting a first-order lens to the homey quarters of screwpile lights with diminutive sixth-order lenses.

The federal lighthouse service, directed by the U.S. Light House Establishment under the Department of the Treasury, was the brainchild of Secretary of the Treasury Alexander Hamilton. Following early decades of mismanagement, in 1852, Congress placed the supervision of the lighthouses under the Light House Board. Nevertheless, lighthouse positions remained entangled politically and points of contention throughout the nineteenth century.

President William Howard Taft disbanded the board in 1910 and established the U.S. Bureau of Lighthouses (U.S. Lighthouse Service) under the Department in Commerce (later the Department of Commerce and

Labor). The bureau raised the professionalism among keepers but curtailed the appointment of white women and Black men. Under the direction of President Franklin Roosevelt, the U.S. Coast Guard took control of the lighthouses in 1939, but civilian keepers continued to serve. This resulted in senior civilian lighthouse keepers directing coast guard seamen who served as assistant keepers. In 1967, the coast guard became part of the Department of Transportation. Thirty-six years later, President George W. Bush transferred the coast guard to the Department of Homeland Security.

As previously mentioned, most of the stations within the boundaries of this book were screwpile lighthouses. This inexpensive structure replaced many lightships and became synonymous with the Chesapeake Bay. Starting in the 1850s, there were four screwpile lights within the area: Craney Island, Deep Water Shoal, White Shoal and Point of Shoal. Others followed after the Civil War. This welcoming design continues to be seen along waterfronts in the architecture of the Hampton Maritime Center, Smithfield Station and the Stingray Point Lighthouse in Deltaville. Likewise, the Rip Rap Brewing Company of Norfolk has made a screwpile lighthouse the centerpiece of its logo.

When the Civil War erupted in 1861, the beacons became targets, and the Confederates darkened all the region's lighthouses, with the exception of the Old Point Comfort Lighthouse. Rebels captured at least one keeper, while some of the former keepers enlisted in the Confederate armed forces. By late 1862, many of these stations were back in federal hands and signaling to ships with temporary beacons. After the conflict, former Confederate and Union service members attended the lights; this included Black men. These Black veterans were part of a larger group of more than twenty-five politically active community leaders. To that point, three Black lighthouse keepers within the scope of this study served in the general assembly.

The passing of the Civil War did not quell the nation's turmoil. During Reconstruction and the peak of the Readjuster epoch (roughly 1879 to 1886), intense political divisions ensnared the lives of many keepers. In 1887, Keeper Milton L. O'Dell of the Cape Henry Lighthouse claimed a party of men attempted to execute him as a form of political suppression. Various means of harassment were also directed at Black lighthouse keepers. This resulted in formal investigations by the Light House Board. The matter of the spoils system was so apparent that naval commander Robley D. Evans, the district head, opposed certain appointments and advised keepers not pay the expected 5 percent of their income to the political party that secured the keepers their respective appointments. Politicians then maneuvered to relieve Evans of his duties.

As if politics and racism did not bring enough strife to lighthouse operations, some keepers became involved in murder trials. One keeper served as an expert witness with relevant information on local tides and geography. The aforementioned O'Dell accused fellow keepers of attempted murder. A third keeper was retained and questioned as a suspect in a murder investigation but was later released. And a fourth individual, Littleton Owens, who served briefly as a keeper, later murdered his estranged wife's lover, only to be pardoned by the governor.

Much like nineteenth-century politics, waterborne excitement sometimes came to those individuals who were standing watch. Yachtsmen employed the stations as racing pylons or finishing lines. The keepers also witnessed naval maneuvers and live fire exercises. The men at Thimble Shoal saw the battleship USS *Missouri* (BB 63) and the presidential yacht *Mayflower* (PY 1) become grounded near their stations. Freezing weather, errant vessels and storms wreaked havoc on the lighthouses. In 1886, many of the keepers even experienced an earthquake. As the twentieth century progressed, the number of stations with resident keepers declined until 1983, when the coast guard automated the Cape Henry Lighthouse, the last station in the commonwealth to quarter permanent keepers.

While many of the stations were dismantled, five structures are still standing: Old Point Comfort, Newport News Middle Ground, Thimble Shoal and both towers of the Cape Henry Station. All of these remaining structures have been recognized for their significance as federal and state landmarks. With that in mind, these silent sentinels have served as majestic backdrops for weddings, ceremonies and momentous events. In an effort to preserve two of these stations, the federal government allowed private interests to purchase at auction the Thimble Shoal and the Newport News Middle Ground Stations, with the expectation that the coast guard would be given access.

Given the popularity of lighthouses, the likenesses of these structures have appeared on postcards, logos, T-shirts, government seals, postage stamps and license plates. In 2001, the Virginia State Lottery Commission offered an Instant Lottery Game 209, featuring lighthouses on the tickets. To no surprise, artists are captivated by the mercurial seascapes that surround these steady beacons. Lighthouses can conjure ghost stories and thoughts of sublime isolation and heart-stopping adventure.

Through the following chapters on individual lighthouses, there is a thread that flows to the next lighthouse. The ebb and flow of fleets, events and the movement of people change like the tides flirting with the stations. Within this setting, a seaside observer with a meandering mind can listen to the motion of the water and conjure sea yarns—no facts are needed. For others, however, who desire to know more about the southeastern Virginia lighthouses, this book should be of interest.

Benjamin H. Trask
Hampton, VA

ACKNOWLEDGEMENTS

There were dozens of individuals who enhanced this project. Many of the contributors were old friends, family members and colleagues, which made the effort even more enjoyable. Along with my associates, the others involved were librarians, archivists, pharologists and historians. I want to acknowledge their respective contributions.

Libraries and archives are great places to start research, so let me start there. My old buddy R. Thomas Crew Jr. assisted me at the Library of Virginia. While in the state capital, I also received help at the Virginia Historical Society. During research respites in Richmond, I enjoyed the engaging company of my nephew Robert T. Bohannon. Closer to home, the staff of the Sargeant Memorial Collection of the Slover Library of Norfolk were very helpful. The staff at the National Archives guided me through the maze of Record Group 26 to learn about the lives of lighthouse keepers. Finally, I especially need to acknowledge the staff the Hampton Public Library's Virginiana Room: Elizabeth Wilson, Marion Jones, Pam Luke and Victoria Ritchson. They filled interlibrary loan requests, answered questions and offered encouragement.

As with my past projects, Peggy Haile-McPhillips, a retired historian for the city of Norfolk, provided advice, served as a reader and shared her great insight on the culture of Hampton Roads. My children, Alex, Gwen and Evan, purchased numerous lighthouse histories, which I requested as presents. The Mariners' Museum staff members Julie Murphy and Lisa M. Williams graciously allowed me to exchange a lighthouse presentation for permission to use their images. George Chakvetadze of Alliance USA skillfully designed the maps used in this book. Barbara G. Bauer, honorary lighthouse keeper at Old Point Comfort, shared stories and images that reflect her affection for this historic treasure. Her husband, Bill Bauer, and Rick Hopson assisted with finding related images.

Katie Arredondo of the Fox Hill Historical Society and Robert Deal told me tales about the Back River Lighthouse. Sheri Hoard provided wise advice with the book proposal. My brother-in-law, Harold W. Bohannon Jr., PE, answered questions related to construction and engineering. Cindy Hudgins Brizzolara of Houston offered background information and documentation on her lighthouse ancestors from Mathews County. Joan and Robert Gonsoulin and Daniel and Jackie Billingsley of the Newport News Middle Ground Lighthouse kindly answered questions and provided information and photographs. My old friend Gregg Vicik came to the rescue with image reproduction and professional photographs of Point Comfort. Brewer 'Liam Bell of the Rip Rap Brewing Company allowed me permission to use the logo of his firm to represent the ubiquitous nature of screwpile lighthouses.

Most importantly, I need to thank acquisition editor Kate Jenkins of The History Press, who was extremely flexible and patient in adjusting the publication schedule around the life of a schoolteacher (i.e. "You're late, Benn.").

CAPE HENRY STATION

Venerable, Attached Friends, 1792

Old Cape Henry Light

There is no greater symbol of hope than a light tower that signals to weary mariners who have crossed tempestuous seas. With that understanding, as early as 1720, colonial officials, such as Virginia's governor Alexander Spotswood, considered the construction of a signal at Cape Henry. Once Virginia and Maryland had constructed the tower, ship masters were to pay a tonnage tax to recover the building and maintenance costs. However, the colonies needed to coordinate their efforts and receive permission from Great Britain before proceeding with the project. In addition, the colonies struggled to convince the powers that be in Great Britain of the added value of a lighthouse.[1]

Vessels transported quarried sandstone from Aquia Creek to Cape Henry in Princess Anne County (later Virginia Beach). Enslaved laborers contributed to this initial effort. The movement of the stone to the future building location proved to be a challenge, as drifting sand threatened to engulf the stone when construction was delayed. Meanwhile, outbuildings were constructed but not the tower.[2]

The American Revolution further delayed construction. The fledgling nation emerged from the conflict deeply in debt. Ironically, it was this debt that provided the impetus to finally finish the project. The first secretary of the treasury, Alexander Hamilton, developed a plan to raise revenue and

Above: The majestic Cape Henry Lighthouse was the last beacon of home observed by mariners when leaving the Chesapeake Bay. *The Mariners' Museum.*

Opposite: As the first secretary of the treasury, Alexander Hamilton (1789–95) was involved with the construction of the first Cape Henry Lighthouse. Hamilton was also part of the discussion for a lighthouse at Old Point Comfort. *Painting by John Trumbull; Wikimedia Commons.*

honor the nation's debts. To do this, Hamilton established the Revenue Cutter Service (the forerunner of the coast guard) to enforce laws related to shipping duties. He also created a marine hospital system to care for seafarers and a lighthouse service to protect ships and their cargo. Hamilton and other notable founding fathers, such as George Washington, Thomas Jefferson and John Jay, showed a keen interest in the construction and administration of lighthouses, such as the one in Cape Henry.[3]

The erection of the Cape Henry Lighthouse became the first light project that was totally supervised by the federal government. In August 1790, Virginia governor Beverly Randolph sent a deed for two acres of land for the undertaking to Hamilton. Out of seven bidders, master builder John McComb Jr. of New York City won the contract and drew the plans for the Cape Henry Lighthouse. McComb later designed two more lighthouses in his native state and built Hamilton's home (now the Alexander Hamilton Grange National Memorial). McComb employed harder stone from Rappahannock quarries in the construction of the 129-foot-tall tapering, octagonal tower.[4]

The project included an oil vault and a wooden keeper's house. The eight lamps burned spermaceti oil and were enhanced by reflectors. Brass wire shielded the glass from birds and hail. On October 2, 1792, McComb completed the project. In the early 1800s, the light was upgraded to hold eighteen Argand lamps with twelve-inch reflectors that projected from a seventy-foot focal plane. These improved lamps included adjustable wicks that required less trimming. Genevan Ami Argand, a chemist and physicist, also added a glass chimney and hollow, cylindrical wicks that increased the air flow and burned brighter.[5]

The Cape Henry Lighthouse's first keeper, William Lewis, served for a year. Other keepers followed in quick succession. When word reached Jefferson that one of these keepers committed a minor offense, he voiced the need to remove the man from office. Jefferson opined, "I think the keepers of lighthouses should be dismissed for small degrees of remissness because of the calamities which even these produce." This expectation was applied, albeit irregularly, to keepers for the generations to follow.[6]

Sliding and Climbing Sandhills, Cape Henry, near Norfolk, Va.

The great sand dunes near Cape Henry were tourist attractions but could make life miserable for the light keepers. This sandy beach front continues south and contributed to the rise of the city of Virginia Beach. *Author's collection.*

In 1799, architect Benjamin H. Latrobe penned detailed a description of the lighthouse's setting. He observed the wetlands, dunes and plank platform that prevented sand from overwhelming the tower. The quarters and oil vault were not so fortunate. The tower was on the tallest dune at the cape, and the continual banking sand placed the tower about 650 yards from the water. The sand even buried the kitchen up to its eaves. Given these conditions, Latrobe concluded the station was "one of the dreariest abodes imaginable." The architect's concerns were not the only hazards in the region.[7]

During the War of 1812, the British Royal Navy regularly cruised coastal Virginia. When the seventy-four-gun HMS *Plantagenet* anchored in Lynnhaven Bay, the crew needed water. With that goal in mind, over the course of a few days, the captain dispatched barges of sailors and marines to dig wells. This activity attracted the Princess Anne County militia. The militia ambushed the landing party, wounding and killing a number of the invaders and setting the remainder scrambling for the *Plantagenet*. During one encounter, Jack Tar raided the keeper's smokehouse before departing. However, the British regularly returned to the bay and Hampton Roads. Rear Admiral George Cockburn directed that frigates "laying well in towards the Sandy Hills under the Light House, and the other laying as near as may be safe to the shoal called the Middle Ground." Consequently, the lighthouse went dark for much of this period.[8]

Once skippers navigated by the dangers of False Cape, the lighthouse served as both a welcoming beacon and marker of departure. Charles Thompson sailed on a brig that left the Virginia Capes with a crew who busied themselves with their respective duties. During the flurry of activity, Thompson spied the captain and a mate "leaning over the rail, gazing at Old Cape Henry Lighthouse, long and earnestly." Likewise, Robert Burts of USS *John Adams* remembered the departure, "We had *logged* our departure from Cape Henry light-house…[as] the pilot had left us with his bag of final letters." Like so many American sailors before and since, Chaplain Walter Colton recalled, as his ship headed for the Mediterranean, the "last object that vanished from my steadfast eye was the old Light House on Cape Henry. I watched *that* as it sunk slowly in the horizon, and felt, when it was gone, as one that has parted with a venerable, attached friend."[9]

Less poetic were the observations of John A. Henriques of New Haven, who served on the schooner *Alcyona*. He was struck by the sand hills and the memory of numerous wrecks along nearby beaches. An example of this type of peril gripped the *Tally Ho*. The ship was bound for Liverpool with cotton, tobacco and flour, when it went ashore west of the lighthouse. The crew was saved, but the vessel was thought to be a total loss. The following year, in the spring of 1841, the brig *Tidal* out of San Juan, bound for Baltimore, went ashore near the lighthouse. The vessel appeared to be a loss, but the crew was able to discharge the cargo.[10]

With the outbreak of the Civil War, the Confederates captured Cape Henry. The Rebels extinguished the light and then conducted a survey of the related property. The well-stocked facility included 180 gallons of sperm oil, four butts (larger than a barrel) of oil, three second-order lamps and various brushes, towels and oil cans. In addition, newspapers outside of the newly formed Confederacy claimed the Rebels lit fires about a mile south of the light to lure ships onto the beach. The *Liverpool Mercury* proclaimed the "British vessel [the *Albion*] is the first to suffer from the lawlessness of the Virginia rebels in removing the coast lights." Notwithstanding, the Union navy remained a dominant force off the Virginia coast. Consequently, the Union established a lightship in one of the bay's shipping channels. However, in January 1862, the vessel broke its anchor and went ashore at Pleasure House Beach, not far from Cape Henry. The Confederates captured the crew and took them to Norfolk. That same spring, the Confederates abandoned their fortifications around Norfolk, and the Union rapidly reestablished itself at the cape.[11]

This renewed federal presence included protecting and relighting the Cape Henry Lighthouse. The Light House Board proudly announced in the *Baltimore Sun* that as of July 15, 1863, the light would be relit, and the "illuminating apparatus consists of a second order Fresnel lens, showing a fixed white light." To protect the beacon, the district provost marshal established a guard detail from units such as the 173rd Pennsylvania and 155th Ohio (national guards or short-term, drafted militia regiments). For the Pennsylvania regiment, the detachment consisted of a noncommissioned officer and about two dozen soldiers who served weekly intervals.[12]

Sandwiched between the conflict, the lighthouse underwent repairs and improvements. In 1857, masons lined the lighthouse with brick for strength, and metallic reflectors were added. It cost $12,000 to build a new iron stairway. The bridge extending from the tower to the keeper's dwelling was broken down and required rebuilding. And the stepladders inside and outside the lantern room were replaced, along with panes of glass in the lantern. By the mid-1800s, iron had begun to replace stone as a construction material.[13]

In 1870, Willis Augustus "Specs" Hodges assumed the duties as the lighthouse's principal keeper. He was one of the first Black men to officially serve as a lightkeeper—although his tenure as was extremely short. Neither Hodges nor the editor of his autobiography, Professor Willard B. Gatewood Jr., discussed Hodges's tenure at the station. Hodges was born a free Black man in Princess Anne County, and his parents provided him with six months of formal education from a white schoolteacher. With that short tutelage and his own determination, he moved north to New York and became the founder of the short-lived newspaper the *Ram's Horn*. This publication drew him into the same circles as fellow abolitionists Frederick Douglass, William Lloyd Garrison and John Brown.[14]

Hodges returned to his native Princess Anne County after the Civil War and served in various government positions thanks to his connections and leadership skills. Starting in December 1867, he served as a county delegate to the new Constitutional Convention. An engraving of the convention in *Frank Leslie's Illustrated Newspaper* (February 15, 1868) featured Hodges in a prominent position. In 1870, Hodges received the appointment as a head keeper but quickly left to be the night inspector of customs at Old Point Comfort. He also ran unsuccessfully for the House of Delegates. Despite this setback, he remained a politically active Republican. Hodges was a delegate at the Republican convention in Hampton that included future Black keepers Littleton Owens, Exum White, Park(er) Charity, John Bradford "Jack" Jones and Shedrack (Shadrack) Tucker.[15]

In November 1880, the aforementioned Owens received an appointment as the first assistant keeper at Cape Henry, replacing Haywood B. Pettigrew, who was transferred to the Craney Island Station. Owens served a session in Richmond and was made the second assistant keeper the following year. He then served a second session. Owens was one of at least four Black lighthouse keepers to serve in the general assembly. The three other keepers were Alexander G. Lee of Old Point Comfort and Thimble Shoal, Edward D. Bland of Jordan Point and Peter J. Carter of Assateague and Cherrystone Bar.[16]

The move of Owens to the general assembly was part of a broader political shift to tenuously align newly enfranchised Black men with the Republicans and Virginian "Readjusters." The Readjusters were part of just one political faction with Republican roots that sought to adjust the state debt downward, bring Black men to the party, share the spoils of appointment to government positions and promote education and civil reforms. Remarkably, one of the Readjustment leaders was former Confederate general and railroad engineer Senator William Mahone. This arrangement was not always harmonious. For instance, the *Norfolk Virginian* appeared to take delight in reporting that Owens and his company were "greatly incensed with white Readjusters," concerning the nomination of a clerk.[17]

In the 1880s, former Confederate general and later senator William Mahone provided patronage to supporters of Virginia's Readjuster movement, including keepers at Cape Henry. *Library of Congress.*

Those with long memories were perplexed by this unusual alliance involving Mahone. At the Battle of the Crater outside of Petersburg, Mahone's division had thwarted the Union advance after the federals literally blew a hole in the Confederate lines using explosives in underground mines. Many of the Confederates in Mahone's old brigade were in the division, adding to the horror. When Black infantrymen who were part of the federal assault were trapped in the pit created by the explosion, they were murdered by Mahone's units as they attempted to surrender. Remarkably, fifteen years later, this strange political pairing resulted in the appointment of more than a dozen Black lighthouse keepers in the state.[18]

At the close of 1881, the Light House Board extinguished the old Cape Henry Lighthouse, and the newly completed iron tower flashed

Factors of Norfolk sold North Carolina cotton to mills in New England and Europe. They were among the supporters for an upgrade to a first-order lens at Cape Henry Lighthouse. *Author's collection.*

across the Atlantic. The older structure was almost one hundred years old, and shipping interests in Virginia and Maryland sought a more powerful beacon. The three keepers then shifted their respective labors to the new location. Still, the magnificent old pharos was to become the backdrop for countless ceremonies, tours and celebrations in the generations following its retirement as a flashing signal. For example, in 1909, President William H. Taft and industrialist Andrew J. Carnegie, as part of the Atlantic Deeper Waterway Association, which sought to improve navigation, enjoyed an oyster roast in the beacon's shadow.[19]

At the close of the 1920s, the Association for the Preservation of Virginia Antiquities (in 2003, the APVA became Preservation Virginia) took steps to enhance the landmark. The society affixed a plaque honoring the first English landing at Cape Henry. For decades, this springtime commemoration attracted large crowds, who listened to politicians, historians, ministers and bands. Through it all, the lighthouse served as an august backdrop. Other moves included getting the federal government to allocate funds for the restoration of the lighthouse. The transfer of the lighthouse and almost two acres of land to the society followed. In this historical spirit, the United States Tobacco Company of Richmond featured the lighthouse in an advertising campaign, with the slogan, "A white flash in a black sky signals the steady character of the coastal sentry. Puffs of cool, sweet smoke bespeak the mild and friendly character of Old Briar Tobacco."[20]

The Great Depression did not deter these festivities. In 1931, President Herbert Hoover and First Lady Lou Henry Hoover were part of the landing day celebrations. The following year, noted newspaper editor and historian Douglas Southall Freeman offered his educated musings at the ceremony and the official dedication of the beacon as a Virginia landmark. At the close of the Depression, the tower was the backdrop for the sesquicentennial celebration of the federal lighthouse service. Broadcast on the radio, the event gathered the U.S. Coast Guard Academy band, Representative Colgate W. Darden Jr., numerous naval and military officers and heads of the lighthouse service Captain Harold D. King and George R. Putman.[21]

Landmark events were not the only times celebrations were attracted to the setting. The site was part of the garden season tours and attracted youth groups, such as 4-H clubs. In 1964, the light became a national historic landmark. In 1989, the coast guard once again returned to Cape Henry for a celebration, this time for the bicentennial of federal lighthouses. The U.S. Postal Service issued a stamp featuring the old lighthouse as part of a series of commemorative stamps. Around this time, the lighthouse became

Erected in 1935, the Cape Henry Memorial commemorates the first English landing in Virginia in April 1907. This celebrated event brought numerous guests to the lighthouses. *Author's collection.*

the site of numerous weddings for those who enjoyed seaside nuptials. With all of this attention, the army allowed visitors to admire the scene dressed in holiday lights, an event that became a tradition in itself.[22]

While the lighthouse projected a celebratory tone, there were concerns about its accessibility due to the dwindling sand level at the base of the structure. Cement that had been added to the structure generated more erosion. By 2003, eight feet of the light's base were exposed. Preservation Virginia launched a study to determine how to protect the landmark and start repairs. As if erosion was not enough of a threat, on August 23, 2011, a Virginia-centered earthquake rumbled through Tidewater. The 5.8-magnitude quake left cracks in the tower and forced the closing of the site. It was not until early October that inspectors determined visitors could return to the lighthouse.[23]

In 2018, Preservation Virginia closed the structure to make stabilizing improvements to save the lighthouse. A joint effort from Preservation Virginia, federal grants, the City of Virginia Beach and private sources provided more than $1 million for the project to prevent erosion and improve access and signage. The following year, Preservation Virginia reopened the tower with a ribbon-cutting ceremony. Related activities included a LEGO lighthouse contest and historic tours. During the COVID-19 pandemic, tours to the lighthouse were closed but reopened in May 2021. The lighthouse's function as a daymark and celebratory beacon continues into the twenty-first century.[24]

NEW CAPE HENRY LIGHTHOUSE

While the retired beacon thrived in its role as a monument, it was the new tower about 350 feet from the old monolith that assumed the role of flashing signals to maritime traffic into the lower Chesapeake Bay. As the centennial anniversary of original Cape Henry Lighthouse approached, there were concerns about cracks in the old tower. Business interests and regional officials also lobbied for a first-order beacon. In Norfolk, the Cotton Exchange passed a resolution supporting the project. And in 1881, according to the *Baltimore Sun*, foreign ship masters were particularly anxious to have an upgraded light at Cape Henry. Congress originally approved $75,000 for the effort, and fourteen companies submitted bids. Morris, Tasker and Company of Philadelphia, with its submission, won the right to carry out the project. However, there were delays and challenges in the undertaking.[25]

This drawing for the base of the new lighthouse at Cape Henry is similar to the actual structure. *Library of Congress.*

Orville E. Babcock supervised the construction. Babcock was a capable engineer and held the temporary rank of brigadier general during the Civil War. He was also a close friend and private secretary to President U.S. Grant. As a member of the president's administration, Babcock became entangled in scandals, and Grant reluctantly removed him from office. Nonetheless, in 1877, still true to his comrade, Grant placed him in the position of inspector of the Fifth District. Babcock's first task at Cape Henry was to oversee the pouring of its massive concrete foundation. Anchored in the concrete were twenty-four wrought-iron bolts, which were to hold the eight-sided lighthouse in place.[26]

The tower consisted of a cast-iron outer shell and an inner wrought-iron cylinder. The tower had an alternating rectangular black and white pattern. There were manholes between the shells. This was the only iron tower built in the area, but the concept became commonplace elsewhere. The lower level stored oil. The oil was raised to the lantern room at the top via a system of ropes and pulleys. Granite steps led up to a massive door with the year of the light's construction inscribed on it in gilded lettering. Behind that door were six stories marked by twenty-six steps each; the light held numerous landings and a service room. The lamp room sparkled with shiny brightwork and a gleaming lens. The seven wicks in the lamp consumed five gallons of oil a night. From this level, keepers could see Cape Henry on the Eastern

As inspector of lighthouses for the Fifth District, Orville E. Babcock oversaw the construction of the second Cape Henry Lighthouse. His later career reflects the political turmoil that ensnared lighthouse keepers. *Wikimedia Commons.*

Shore. The light's focal plane was 152 feet, and it flashed a white light over 270 degrees that could be seen by vessels more than 18 nautical miles away. Despite issues with its construction, on the evening of December 15, 1881, the light shone for the first time.[27]

In 1886, First Assistant Keeper Phillip Morrisett provided a tour to an unidentified visitor who later described the experience in the *Democratic Advocate*. The article mentioned the nice parlor with a white interior, a Brussels carpet, a lounge under a window, a pair of comfortable chairs and a bookshelf. The watch room included a desk, a marine clock, a telephone and telegraph equipment. Morrisett recalled to the tourist the recent August evening when the Charleston earthquake rumbled through Virginia. He was on watch when the shocks "nearly dislodged the lamp and made him feel lonely."[28]

The year 1887 began with more chaos when a deadly snowstorm overwhelmed the German ship *Elizabeth*, which was wrecked about twelve miles south of the cape. Attempts by the brave men at the lifesaving station resulted in the loss of additional lives. That summer, a thunderstorm struck the cape. Lightning splintered the signal flag pole, hit the signal station and ignited signal flags in the attic. One bolt knifed into the sand and hissed much like a hot blade being quenched in water. At the lighthouse proper, the strike stunned Keeper Milton L. O'Dell, knocking him to the ground, but no serious injuries were sustained.[29]

That fall, O'Dell's problems continued with an investigation that involved his professional behavior. His accusers claimed he misappropriated lighthouse stores, tormented his fellow keepers, played an active role in the Republican Party and was absent from the station during the storm that wrecked the *Elizabeth*. Lighthouse officials convened at the customshouse in Norfolk to hear testimony. Among the group that described O'Dell's role at a Republican rally was former keeper Littleton Owens. After listening to the witnesses and reviewing the evidence, the board, according to the *Norfolk Virginian*, "recommended that the charges be dismissed."[30]

In December, there was an alleged murder attempt on Keeper O'Dell near the lighthouse. According to the keeper, while he was returning to the station, the would-be assailants fired from concealed positions. The *Evening Star* claimed that, owing "to the partisan feeling which Odell [*sic*] thought existed between him and the parties who preferred the [aforementioned] charges, he says he had provided himself with a pair of revolvers to be ready for any emergency." O'Dell declared he returned fire and thought he wounded one of the men. Among the five defendants were First Assistant

Keeper George R. Gwynn and former assistant keepers James B. Hawkins and Phillip Morrisett. O'Dell later displayed bullet holes in his coat and responded that his frightened horse prevented him from pursuing his assailants. The Democratic Party mouthpiece the *Norfolk Virginian* retorted that "there was little evidence against the gentlemen accused. And true to form, the defendants were found not guilty." Following his claims against the trio, O'Dell was charged with perjury and required to pay bail of $300, but a week later, the charges were dismissed.[31]

Through all the political infighting at the station, the light continued to shine. Schooner skipper Leonard S. Tawes recalled a blustering snowy Christmas Day when he headed for what he hoped was Cape Henry. Then, at sunset, Tawes rejoiced, "I sure enough made Cape Henry Lighthouse and I do not know of anything in this world that gave me more releif [*sic*] for I was now sure of getting in the bay." Not long after, Tawes's personal experience with the lighthouse, given in the magazine *Our Navy*, described the beacon as a massive tower that welcomed sailors back to Hampton Roads. He touted that by night, the light could be seen from twenty-four miles away.[32]

Manning the all-important beacon were men such as Keeper William E. Howell. According to the *Blue Book of American Shipping* (1903), he was also a marine engineer. In the 1890s, his movements from the lighthouse to Norfolk were often reported in the press. In addition, he became a spokesman for "Take U-No Tonic, Honduras Famous Blood Purifier." There was a branch office of the elixir company on Main Street in Norfolk. For the price of a quarter, stomach and blood disorders could be cured. Howell's specific ailment was neuralgia that was so bad he "could hardly see." In 1903, the colorful Howell was removed from office as a keeper.[33]

The same year Howell was removed, Petro Beloso arrived at Cape Henry as the first assistant lighthouse keeper. He remained at this post until his death sixteen years later. Unlike most of his fellow keepers, he was a naturalized citizen, having immigrated to the United States in 1839 during a time of much uncertainty on the Italian peninsula. He settled in Little Italy near Fell's Point in Baltimore and worked as a ship's fireman. Before Cape Henry, he tended lights at Smith's Point and Craighill Front Channel. Like Charles W. Vette of Newport News's Middle Ground and Olaf A. Olsen of Nansemond River, Beloso was one of a few immigrants who worked at lighthouses in southeastern Virginia.[34]

The logical companion to a first-order light was a first-class steam-powered fog signal, another laboratory experimentation for the service. A building unto itself, the contraption had a Seussian appearance, complete with horns.

At various times, Cape Henry included a lighthouse, foghorns, weather and wireless telegraph stations and the Virginia pilot tower. *The Mariners' Museum.*

The sound signal gave a 5-second blast with a 90-second break before giving another 5-second blast. In 1893, the signal operated for 256 hours and consumed thirteen tons of coal. The signal was updated to a compressed air system, but two signals were kept in operation for redundancy. In 1911, the *Baltimore Sun* reported that both signals "broke down because of demand for their deep notes during the recent attack of fog on the approaches to the Chesapeake." Given the signals' importance, the lighthouse service quickly repaired both.[35]

In 1908, Assistant Keeper Grover C. Riggs transferred to Cape Henry to work alongside his father, Ephraim Riggs, who assumed the duties as keeper the previous year. The younger Riggs resigned in a few years, but the senior Riggs remained at his assignment. Both men were natives of the Outer Banks. Around this same time, Ephraim Riggs visited another son in western North Carolina, where the keeper was interviewed by a reporter with the *Asheville Gazette-News*. Riggs had been in service for more than twenty years and started his career at Cape Hatteras. Riggs aspired to be the keeper at the Diamond Shoals Lighthouse. However, this project was decades in delay. Riggs remained at Cape Henry for the rest of his life. In 1922, he died in the fog signal room.

During his interview with the Asheville journalist, Riggs mentioned that the Cape Henry Lighthouse was not powered by electricity, because the energy source "had proved too uncertain" for that station. At Cape Henry, coal oil was the fuel of choice. It burned in a configuration of wicks, some being five inches in diameter. In 1910, the district upgraded the kerosene

Surrounded by the massive first-order lens, an unidentified keeper changes bulbs at the Cape Henry Light. *Photograph by Ralph Smith, The Mariners' Museum.*

lamps to oil vapor lamps, which boosted the light to twenty-two thousand candlepower. As the twentieth century began, the Cape Henry Lighthouse did convert to electricity and became a setting for numerous experiments to improve maritime navigation, communication and safety.

In 1914, the federal government acquired more than one thousand acres of land on the cape to erect Fort Story. Construction was slow. This was the newest installation of the coastal defenses of the lower Chesapeake Bay. This step surrounded the lighthouse with a military installation at the beginning of World War I. Despite the army's presence, the pair of lighthouses became the most visited stations in the district, welcoming more than ten thousand visitors each year.[36]

In 1921, Assistant Superintendent Frederick C. Hingsburg took steps to replace the five-wick lamps with filament electric lamps. When electricity was added, the power actually became eighty thousand candlepower. Hingsburg also installed an automatic device that, using a thermostat, replaced burned-out bulbs. This appliance could also signal to the keepers that the replacement bulb needed to be replaced. The improved Cape Henry Lighthouse signaled three flashes every twenty seconds. The first and

Named in honor of General John P. Story in 1914, Fort Story was established by the U.S. Army and surrounded the Cape Henry Light Station. The army still controls access to the two beacons. *The Mariners' Museum.*

Cape Henry has long been a great attraction. This image from 1885 shows visitors that were then able to view two lighthouses. *Photograph by Jared A. Smith, The Mariners' Museum.*

second flashes lasted one second, and the third flash lasted seven seconds. The light also had a red sector. The red-colored glass of the signal room showed a crimson light with twenty-four thousand candlepower. This was warning to mariners that they were on a dangerous course. Cape Henry was a showpiece station, it was natural that during the annual meeting of district superintendents in 1924, the managers took a field trip out to the light to examine the innovations there.[37]

Among the devices tested at the cape by the Lighthouse Bureau were a radio beacon and a foghorn for direction finding. The concept worked thusly: a radio signal from the station could reach a ship at sea instantaneously, while a fog signal, sent at the same moment, would travel the speed of sound (about five and a half seconds for a nautical mile). So, when a fog signal and a radio signal were transmitted simultaneously, with the proper equipment, a ship's navigation officer could learn how far the vessel was from the lighthouse, even in bad weather. Later experiments with this system were upgraded from using spark-gap to vacuum tube transmitters. The latter used less power and experienced less transmission interference.[38]

This innovative navigation system garnered national attention. An article in the *Dayton Daily News* discussed how the system was pioneered and applied at Cape Henry. A photograph's caption read, "Isaac L. Meekins, veteran keeper of the Cape Henry Lighthouse, inspects the dual set of clocks on the panel of beacon timing equipment and synchronous foghorn signals." Under the direction of district engineers, the advancement allowed lightkeepers to bring additional safety to shipping. The outbreak of World War II brought an end to the experiments and the beginning of tremendous changes at Cape Henry. Artillery batteries at the fort conducted live fire exercises, and notices warned mariners to steer clear of the impact zone.[39]

After the war, the coast guard resumed its experiments to improve navigation at the cape. The application of the work of Dr. Harold Edgerton of the Massachusetts Institute of Technology found its way to Virginia. In 1966, a xenon flash with two elongated reflectors was installed at Cape Henry. The two reflectors sent a beam in all directions, and the intensity of the signal could be adjusted based on the weather conditions. Following the experiments, crews reinstalled the first-order Fresnel lens.[40]

At the close of 1983, the lighthouse was automated. The radio beacon system had already been updated with the same thought in mind. The move cost more than $100,000 but was implemented to save money in the long run. Petty Officer First Class Benjamin Stagge, Petty Officer Third Class John Harmon and Fireman Douglas Thompson were the last keepers

The old and new towers of Cape Henry, shown here around 1910, became the focus of countless postcards. *Author's collection.*

in Virginia's last station with a permanent residence. Interviewed by the press, the coast guardsmen noted their sadness of the passing of manned lighthouses, but they took the change in stride.[41]

Even after the departure of keepers, experiments continued at the station. The Connecticut-based FuelCell Energy Incorporation helped develop a 250-kilowatt direct fuel cell powered by coal mine gas emissions (methane), a byproduct of mining. The company's expectations were to reduce greenhouse gas emissions. The firm won a $100,000 grant from the coast guard and, in 2001, planned to test the three-kilowatt fuel cell power system (with methanol) at the Cape Henry Lighthouse. Among this technological development, Preservation Virginia has expressed its desire to also acquire the new tower. This would certainly make this pair of historic beacons another great attraction for pharologists and beach tourists.[42]

2

OLD POINT COMFORT

The "Blessing of Thousands," 1804

The Old Point Comfort Light Station is an anomaly. The life of a keeper is often characterized by hardship and isolation. Instead, the history of this quaint station at the end of the Virginia Peninsula has long been the opposite of this scenario. The setting could be considered idyllic. Case in point, in the serial story "White Squadron Tales," set at Old Point, the author mused that the "stillness of the balmy autumnal night had fallen on land and sea. The moon now riding high in the heavens showered a path of liquescent silver over the waters: the winking eye of the Thimble light house gleamed now and again from out the velvety darkness seaward." Interestingly, the setting was Old Point, while the distant Thimble Shoal Lighthouse accented the romantic evening.[43]

Generations earlier, however, the locale was lonely. In May 1774, John Dames petitioned the House of Burgesses for maintaining a beacon light with a stipend for his services. He was to be paid from the funds that had been set aside to build a light tower at Cape Henry. As early as 1775, state officials paid twenty pounds a year to maintain a signal at Old Point. Still, it was not until after the American Revolution that a serious discussion emerged for a permanent tower.

In 1803, Elzy Burroughs, an experienced stonemason and builder, finished most of the forty-four-foot-tall, octagonal, white, tapered tower. A stone spiral stairway leads to the metal ladder beneath the trapdoor of the lantern room. Four windows flank the stairway. A dull, red, domed copper roof with a lightning rod tops the structure. In the fall of 1804, the lantern room caught fire. Newspapers such as the *National Intelligence* noted the damage reports and declared the "Light house on Old Point Comfort, at the entrance of the Chesapeake, was a few days since, destroyed by fire." A captain who landed in New England detailed in the *Windham Herald* that the losses included oil, copper and lead needed for repairs and mirrors (reflectors). Soon, the needed repairs were made, and the light went back online.[44]

During the War of 1812, no fort shielded the beacon. Observers from the lighthouse could see British naval fleets that sailed into the Chesapeake Bay, such as Rear Admiral George Cockburn's flotilla. The American contingent on Craney Island at the mouth of the Elizabeth River checked the invaders' attempt to take Norfolk. Angry about the setback, the British torched Hampton and departed. When the fighting passed, the lighthouse lamps were relit, but the British returned to the bay. At the close of 1814, an unidentified American captain climbed the tower to make the following observation about the enemy: "I have this moment returned from the Old Point Comfort Light House where I have been to view the movement of the British vessels." Captain John S. Skinner sent a similar-sounding dispatch to Secretary of the Navy William Jones. If this were the case, it is unlikely that Skinner was the actual scout who spied from the lighthouse.[45]

The British naval presence in Hampton Roads during the Revolution and the War of 1812 prompted the federal government to erect a series of coastal forts. Two of them would protect the harbor: Forts Monroe and Calhoun (renamed Fort Wool in 1862). Secretary of War John C. Calhoun (1782–1850), the namesake of Fort Calhoun, was a South Carolinian and supporter of slavery and states' rights. Consequently, during the Civil War, the Union renamed Fort Calhoun in honor of Union general John Wool. In 1818, engineers began to expand the lighthouse pier. It was later known as Engineer Wharf. With the quay upgraded, stone began to arrive for the construction of Fort Monroe. Offshore, riprap created an artificial island that became the foundation for Fort Calhoun. Meanwhile, there was a discussion about moving the lighthouse during the fort's construction, but the relocation of the tower did not occur.[46]

Alongside the fortifications, around 1822, entrepreneurs built a hotel. The Hygeia Hotel eventually attracted the antebellum elite, including politicians such as Henry Clay, Andrew Jackson, John Tyler and Millard Fillmore. At the close of 1862, the army required the removal of the hotel. However, after the war, two notable hotels flourished, the second Hygeia Hotel and the Hotel Chamberlain. The second Hygeia Hotel later closed, and in 1920, the Chamberlain caught fire. By the end of the Jazz Age, a second Hotel

Chamberlain stood in its place. All of these proximate hostelries made living at the lighthouse compelling.[47]

By the mid-1800s, the Old Point Lighthouse required eleven oil lanterns with fourteen-inch reflectors. Soot often fouled the glass panes. The signal consumed 486 gallons of oil annually. Keeper William C. King, a former shoe store manager, operated the light. In 1854, the station was modernized with a fourth-order Fresnel lens. The focal plane was forty-five feet, and it could be observed eleven and a half nautical miles away. And once again, the Department of the Treasury considered moving the tower and even provided funds for "removing the lighthouse at Old Point Comfort into Fortress Monroe." Efforts to construct a tall, wooden fog bell were delayed by the yellow fever epidemic that ravaged Norfolk. The bronze bell itself was forty inches in diameter and thirty-six inches tall. In 1855, foundry workers at Henry Hooper & Co. in Boston cast the signal. The tower was rebuilt at least twice before it was permanently removed from the station. With the aid of a northwest breeze, the ringing could be heard three miles away.[48]

From 1857 to 1861, Amelia Dewees served as the principal keeper. Her salary—and that of other female keepers of the time—was comparable to that of her male counterparts. Unlike most female keepers, she was not the widow of a keeper. In addition, her son Robert A. Dewees served briefly as the assistant keeper. A female supervisor in the lighthouse service was noteworthy but not unique. Dewees appears to have been the first appointed female keeper (principal or assistant) in the greater Hampton Roads area. She was part of an American tradition of female civilian keepers, who continued to serve until the mid-twentieth century. Simultaneously, across the globe, women served as keepers in Canada, the United Kingdom, France, New Zealand and Australia. In the 1870s, the number of women keepers peaked nationally. In the Hampton Roads region, most of the local women worked as assistants, with their respective husbands serving as head keepers.[49]

When South Carolina departed from the Union in December 1860, other states of the Deep South followed. Virginians anxiously monitored the exodus. This schism placed Keeper Dewees in a predicament. Her son, machinist and former assistant keeper joined the Confederate army as part of the Hampton Grays of the Thirty-Second Virginia Infantry. Shortly thereafter, she resigned or was removed from her post. In 1863, Sergeant Dewees, listed as a deserter, was transported to Fort Monroe, took an oath of allegiance and was released. The twenty-two-year-old then rejoined his old unit and was paroled again in Richmond at the end of the war. Amelia Dewees appears to have worked as a seamstress until her death in August

The headstone of Amelia Dewess (died in 1865) at St. John's Church Cemetery. She may have been the first female principal keeper in the area. *Author's collection.*

The expansive beachfront showing Old Point Comfort Lighthouse during the Civil War. Later, the army erected guns in front of the light tower. *Library of Congress.*

1865 at the age of forty-seven. She was buried at St. John's Episcopal Church in Hampton.[50]

The lighthouse, shielded by Union-held Fort Monroe, remained in federal control, unlike other regional lighthouses and lightships. Hampton Roads flourished as a Union staging area for amphibious operations down the southeastern coast. Consequently, the Old Point Comfort Lighthouse was needed. Flag Officer Louis M. Goldsborough recommended to Fort Monroe's commanding officer General John Wool that sections of the light be shuttered so that Confederates near Norfolk would not benefit from its illumination. After the fighting, travelers once again roamed the point and

Artist E.A. Christie was known for her seascapes. Painted in 1871, this view shows the coast of Old Point Comfort before the seawall was constructed to protect it against erosion. *The Mariners' Museum.*

examined all of its attractions. The imprisonment of the former Confederate president Jefferson Davis in a casemate within the fort's moat added to the importance of the installation. Davis was to be tried for treason in federal court. After being released on bond, he was never brought to trial.[51]

In 1869, the *Richmond Dispatch* relayed the findings that stated the "beacon light at this station [Old Point Comfort], being no longer of any service to navigation, has been discontinued." Nevertheless, official reports note the facility's outbuildings; whitewashed kitchen, fences and tower; glass set; painted window frames and sashes; and cistern were cleaned and given a new coat of cement, and its floors were re-laid. In addition, its plaster was repaired, "most of which has been shaken down by the concussion caused by heavy guns." The Union's twelve-inch rifled and fifteen-inch Rodman guns that were mounted in front of the station and fired rounds that weighed more than four hundred pounds could have been responsible for the fallen plaster. Robert K. Sneden, a topographical engineer in the Fortieth New York, detailed in his diary that he saw "several [unmounted] monster guns near the lighthouse at the point."[52]

Coastal guns positioned in front of the lighthouse after the Civil War stood ready to protect the harbor during two world wars. *Author's collection.*

Once back in service, the station continued to see improvements. In 1884, army surveyors furnished cornerstones of the property and noted the light tower was flanked by the keeper's quarters, three outbuildings to the south and a fog bell tower closer to the water. The surveyors determined almost all of the structures fell within the original land survey of 1799. Various outbuildings were added, including a small stable, 420 feet of wooden fence, iron railings and a new oil house. Congress also later appropriated funds for the keeper's house to be placed on a sewage line that was to be maintained by the post quartermaster. Finally, to keep the often-visited grounds attractive, fifty carts of topsoil and sixty-three assorted plants were distributed on the grounds. The old keeper's dwelling (built around 1823) was rebuilt. The rear stairs allowed the assistant keeper to enter the second floor. In 1980, the post's environmental officer Phyllis Sprock, who inventoried the home, described it thus: "Stylistically the building exhibits influences from the Shingle Style of the 1870s…a touch of Queen Anne, and soupçon of Eastlake [architect Charles Eastlake]."[53]

During these upgrades and later, three Black men served as the light's principal keeper: Reverend William Roscoe Davis (1870–78), John "Jack" Bradford Jones (1878–1908) and William Wright Jones (1908). Alexander G. Lee served briefly as an assistant. John Jones had served as a steward in the U.S. Navy and sergeant in the Thirty-Eighth Colored Infantry during the Civil War. Davis was born into slavery and led an incredible life. In Norfolk, Davis's owner taught him to read and write and later moved him to Hampton. He was a pleasure boat skipper who could be hired by hotel guests. Early in the Civil War, Davis followed the pattern of thousands of enslaved people and fled to Fort Monroe. More than a keeper, Davis emerged as a political and religious leader in Hampton.[54]

A.P. Davis, the grandson of William R. Davis Jr., recalled stories of his father, who lived at the lighthouse. According to these accounts, during an inspection, a haughty naval officer, while examining the keeper's quarters, was quick to give orders on running the station. Davis checked the officer with the remark that while the station belonged to the government, the inspector was in Davis's house. The officer paused, slowly removed his cover and apologized. The keeper's quarters also became an entertainment hub for Black people to enjoy the beach in front of the lighthouse. Davis's grandson recalled his "grandfather [Walter R. Davis] lost his job when his political faction went out of power." In 1878, the Democratic-leaning *Norfolk Landmark* simply recorded that Davis was "removed" from office. John Jones then became the principal keeper.[55]

Before Jones became a head keeper, he served as an Elizabeth City County (Hampton) delegate at a local Republican Party convention. Jones and his wife, Sallie Tazewell Jones, arrived at the station with a large family that only grew. The enterprising John Jones also apparently owned dairy cows and was a meat carver at a nearby hotel. Through these outside opportunities, he amassed considerable personal wealth and still maintained his status as a reliable keeper in politically turbulent times.[56]

Jones quickly negotiated a raise in 1880, from $500 to $600 per annum. Commander George Dewey noted, "Inspector reports Mr. Jones to be efficient keeper whose duties merit an increase of pay." This could be considered quite an endorsement, as Dewey later became an admiral in the United States Navy. Justification for the raise at this "important station" included the lack of an assistant and "constantly attending to the light and fog bell." In addition, "there are a great many visitors, which requires a good deal of extra labor." Jones got the raise and even briefly directed Lee as an assistant.[57]

In the fall of 1877, the Elizabeth City County (Hampton) electorate picked Alexander G. Lee to be their delegate in the general assembly. Later, the Light House Board appointed Lee as an assistant at Thimble Shoal and then Jones's first assistant keeper at Old Point Comfort at a salary of $440 a year.

The Hotel Chamberlain around 1900, when Principal Keeper John B. Jones of Old Point Comfort may have also worked as a meat carver at the resort. *Author's collection.*

The seawall at Old Point Comfort, as seen from the bell tower, circa 1915, showing the Hotel Chamberlain. *Library of Congress.*

The back of the keeper's house at Old Point Comfort. The assistant keeper resided upstairs. *Author's collection.*

Lee's tenure as a keeper was marked with controversy and brought him into conflict with the district inspector Commander Robley D. Evans. On the other hand, Sallie Jones also helped operate the lighthouse; the census of 1900 listed her as an assistant keeper. This acknowledgement of her contribution in running the lighthouse by the census enumerator was quite unusual. This made her one of two Black women so recognized in the region.[58]

In the mid-1880s, as the influence of the Readjusters declined, Jones became the target of a petition to remove him from office. The complaint claimed that his various political activities took the keeper away from his primary duties. A subsequent investigation conducted by district inspector Commander Robley D. Evans concluded that "the charges seem to me frivolous.…J.B. Jones has no doubt been a Republican, but there is nothing to show that he has done anything to warrant his removal from the lighthouse service. All testimony is to the effect that he is an excellent keeper, to which I may add my own that he is a faithful and efficient public servant." Likewise, army ordnance officer Major Lawrence S. Babbitt professed he had known Jones for six years and believed "this man Jno. Jones to be sober and reliable…and unassuming."[59]

Jones weathered this political storm, only to experience a different type of turbulence the following year. On a calm evening at the end of August 1886, Keeper Jones noticed a sudden rise in the bay's water. He also felt tremors and heard rumblings for about two minutes. The motion was strong enough to neutralize the harmonics of a two-foot clock pendulum. The timepiece stopped at 9:55 p.m. The epicenter of this disturbance was coastal South Carolina and became known as the Charleston earthquake. The earthquake (estimated at 7.6 magnitude), one of the most powerful recorded earthquakes to emanate from the East Coast, started in earnest about four minutes before Jones felt its tremors. The shaking rattled crockery, swayed lamps and cracked ceilings in higher-level buildings in Hampton.[60]

In January 1908, John Jones died. His obituary in the *Evening Star* of Washington, D.C., claimed "his record for efficiency was excellent." The *Daily Press* remarked he was "widely known in Tidewater, Virginia," had been recommended for the position by future rear admiral Evans and "held the position…even through the two administrations of Grover Cleveland [a Democrat] as President." The *Washington Bee*, a Black-owned paper, noted Jones "left property valued at $25,000 made by working at times which did not interfere with his duties as lighthouse keeper." Following Jones's death, his son William Jones served briefly at the light.[61]

Just before the United States entered World War I, the lighthouse service began to readjust the fog bell, which stood at about the same height as the light tower. The now electrically operated bell was moved closer to Engineers Wharf. The signal sounded every seven and a half seconds and rested about 170 yards from the lighthouse. In 1921, the *Baltimore Sun* noted the signal's relocation "has been confusing mariners making the Point," so it was again relocated farther away from the light before it was removed. During World War I, veteran keeper Elijah A. Hozier died in his quarters, having served a decade at the station. The *Daily Press* reported that he "filled this important station with untiring energy and faithfulness."[62]

The new century ushered in other modern improvements and modifications. First, in 1919, the United States Lighthouse Service switched from oil to electric incandescent power for the fourth-order lens. The apparatus then projected a beam with the intensity of 3,300 candlepower. With the arrival of manned flight, authorities at the Department of Commerce looked to get double duty out of their light stations. The structures would be not only seamarks but also landmarks for aerial navigators. Certain houses were to have their roofs painted with designations so airplane pilots could trace their flights paths from Norfolk

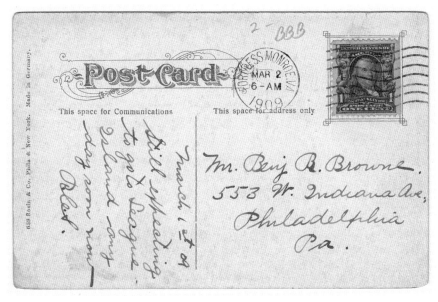

Apparently, a sailor from the Great White Fleet marked the location where his returning vessel anchored near the Old Point Comfort Light. He anticipated steaming to League Island, Philadelphia. *Author's collection.*

Old Point Comfort Lighthouse around the end of Keeper John B. Jones's long tenure at the station. *Author's collection.*

and Washington, D.C. Old Point Comfort, Thimble Shoal and Newport News's Middle Ground were to be marked in this proposed chain.[63]

Other experimenters studied "the practicability of using a light beam to automatically start and stop a fog signal at the beginning and ending of poor visibility conditions." On October 18, 1936, electricians installed the network. The battery-powered light flashed from Fort Wool to the station. The photoelectric beam shone for two seconds every two minutes onto a photoelectric cell. When changes in the atmosphere (snow, fog or rain) disrupted the beam, the bell sounded. The mechanism was installed for test purposes, and inspectors' reports do not reveal how long the switch remained in service.[64]

In the 1930s, keepers were expected to provide lighthouse tours. Keeper George G. Johnson was to give tours six days a week, including on Sunday afternoons. One of the interesting features of the station was the small warning bell located on the second floor of the keeper's home connected with the light. When the bulb darkened, a signal rang to Johnson to replace the bulb. Johnson was also to relay to the keepers at Thimble Shoal Lighthouse if distressed mariners near the point needed assistance. This was necessary, because there were no small craft attached to the Old Point Lighthouse.[65]

In the summer of 1941, much of the planet was entangled in World War II, but the neutrality of the United States allowed for New London to Old Point Comfort sailing races. The races were sponsored in part by the Hampton Yacht Club, and the lighthouse was the finish line. When the Japanese

Old Point Comfort Lighthouse and the expanded Engineers Wharf. The original pier at this location served the light station. *The Mariner's Museum.*

Originally, Fort Wool (Calhoun) was to work in concert with Fort Monroe to create an artillery crossfire to enemy ships trying to enter the harbor. *Author's collection.*

U. S. BATTLESHIP FLEET BY NIGHT. HAMPTON ROADS.

OLD POINT COMFORT. VA.   46227

This dramatic image of Old Point Comfort Lighthouse around the 1930s. Eventually, the nearby coastal lights competed with the lighthouse's signal light. *Author's collection.*

attack on Pearl Harbor jolted America into the global conflict, there was tremendous activity at Old Point Comfort. Batteries of ninety-millimeter antiaircraft guns blazed during firing exercises that extended twenty thousand yards offshore. The U.S. Navy acquired the Hotel Chamberlain for living quarters. The authorities removed the two cupolas on top of the hotel and replaced them with antiaircraft emplacements. The cupolas were never replaced. Civilian movement to the forts and Hampton Roads were sharply restricted, and the army planted mines and antisubmarine netting as a defensive measure. Keeper George G. Johnson, a veteran of the lighthouse service for more than forty years, and a coast guardsman, Fireman First Class Bill Olander, tended to the beacon throughout the war.[66]

Following the conflict, the prewar levels of illumination returned to Point Comfort and competed with the lighthouse. Therefore, in 1954, electricians implemented a test at the station. Five 250-watt bulbs on poles were extended from the guardrails just below the lens like spokes from a hub to distinguish the signal. Keeper William J. Clark, one of the last civilian lighthouse keepers, thought this might make the Old Point Comfort Lighthouse signal more distinct. Sadly, the noble lighthouse looked more like an amusement park ride that could have been found at Buckroe Beach. Soon thereafter, the light resumed its more conventional configuration.[67]

50

With the war over, activities at the post became more relaxed. Keeper Clark and his coast guard assistant, Seaman Bob F. West, toiled at the light's workshop, making the scenery for a production of *Maria Marten* that was performed at the fort's YMCA. Set in England, the tale is also known as *Red Barn Murder*. On a calmer note, teachers at the post's elementary school led field trips to the light. Other sightseers included Boy Scouts, Brownies, tourists, army personnel and artists. The smooth steps curving tightly along stone walls may have given visitors the sensation of climbing up a castle tower. On the other hand, head keeper Chief Boatswain's Mate John Arnett likened it to residing in an oyster shell. The tours stopped around January 1973, after the light was automated.[68]

The coast guard then turned the keeper's house over to the army to serve as the residence of the post's command sergeant major. Not long after the transfer, a disturbing tale was told by residents and guests who saw a table collapse, even though its supports were not moved by anyone. Later, many of the same guests saw spoons mysteriously fly from the same table at another gathering. In context of the lore of Old Point Comfort, this comes as no surprise. The installation features a stretch of road called "ghost alley." There is a rambling pet cemetery along the fort's parapets. Sergeant Major

A mid-twentieth-century view of the Old Point Comfort Lighthouse with two keepers assigned to the station. *The Mariners' Museum.*

Edgar A. Perry, better known as Edgar Allan Poe, served at the post and later returned to Old Point Comfort for readings at the hotel. In addition, there are numerous tales of hauntings at the fort and the Chamberlain Hotel. So, creepy stories about the keeper's quarters only seem fitting.[69]

In 1999, national media attention focused on the undertaking to relocate North Carolina's Cape Hatteras Lighthouse. Barbara G. Bauer of Hampton then decided the Old Point Comfort Lighthouse should also be recognized. She also served as a hostess for the lighthouse at several "Mistletoe Tours" offered by Fort Monroe during the holiday season. Following Thanksgiving, she decorated the tower with garland and a huge wreath for the Christmas season. In the spring of 2002, she arranged a one-day open house with the help of coast guard auxiliary (Flotilla 61) that was a big success. A steady line of lighthouse seekers continued throughout the day and demonstrated their interest in the oldest active lighthouse on the Chesapeake Bay. Along with the sights, tales of memorable childhood outings, as well as first kisses and weddings, were shared by the public that day. Bauer's diligence earned her the title "honorary lighthouse keeper" from the Fifth District headquarters. Unfortunately, the coast guard's concerns about the structure and its exposure to mold and other hazards terminated Bauer's tenure.

With the closure of Fort Monroe as an active military installation by the Base Realignment and Closure Commission, starting in 2005, the keeper's house was then made available for renting. While performing her duties at the beacon, a resident near the structure approached "Keeper" Bauer about a mysterious woman wearing a long dress in the tower. Honorary keeper Bauer continued to be a conduit for these reports as residents in the keeper's house moved in and out of the home. Bauer recalled these eerie snippets convinced her of the validity of these "ghost stories." The tales relayed to her included sightings of books sliding across a table and the spirit of a child appearing above a sleeper's bed.[70]

Bauer was more than a collector of stories and a window washer. She maintained flower beds and learned the station's history.[71]

As for the automated lighthouse, it flashed a signal: two seconds dark, two seconds light and six seconds dark. The white beam covered 132 degrees. The rest of the circle showed a red signal, indicating to the vessel that could see the steady red light that it was on a dangerous course. At the same time, the significance of the lighthouse began to be acknowledged. The site was listed in the Virginia Landmarks Register and National Register of Historic Places. Likewise, in the spring of 1989, Colonel Eugene F. Scott, the post commander, hosted a ceremony to dedicate a historic marker telling the story of the lighthouse.[72]

Above: Tours of the Old Point Comfort Lighthouse in May 2002, organized by Barbara Bauer. *Courtesy of Barbara Bauer.*

Left: The fourth-order lens of the Old Point Comfort Lighthouse. The darkened (red) plexiglass is to notify mariners that their present course is not in the channel and their vessel may be in danger. *Courtesy of Barbara Bauer.*

Behind the Old Point Comfort Lighthouse is the moat that was built in front of the original stone fort. *Photograph by Gregg Vicik.*

The Old Point Comfort Lighthouse
with Fort Wool in the background.
Photograph by Gregg Vicik.

In the summer of 2019, a cornerstone event in American history was formally acknowledged at Old Point Comfort. Four hundred years earlier, the first Africans had been forcibly transported to Virginia. At the time of their landing, all vessels destined for Jamestown were required to stop at Fort Algernourne at the Point. This was the first step toward the enslavement of Africans in British North American colonies, and it has since become a day of remembrance at the Fort Monroe National Monument.

In 2020, another epic event rippled through the roadstead. On a beautiful spring day, citizens lined the fort's seawall to witness the departure of the USNS *Comfort* (T-AH-20) for New York City during the COVID-19 pandemic. The hospital ship returned a month later. This spontaneous celebration harkened back to George Washington's birthday in 1909, when the Great White Fleet returned. On this occasion, the *Daily Press* exclaimed the "shore line was black with a path of umbrellas from the wharf at Old Point Comfort to the Fort Monroe light." In both instances, naval vessels returned, and the Old Point Comfort Lighthouse welcomed them back to Hampton Roads.[73]

3

BACK RIVER

Reflections and Shadows, 1829

Built on the Chesapeake Bay, Back River Lighthouse functioned for more than a century in obscurity—with the exception of one event. This singular happenstance was not a gale, a shipwreck or a battle. This tragedy unfolded on a balmy summer's day in the early years of the Great Depression within the "shadow" of the small lighthouse, and it involved the demise of a young socialite. That much is agreed on. The controversy around her demise can best be explained with a question: Was the cause of her death an accident, natural causes or murder?

The history of the lighthouse itself began more than a century earlier, on March 29, 1829, when the federal government purchased a four-acre square of land south of the Back River in Elizabeth City County (present-day Hampton) for $100 and made an additional smaller acquisition for a drainage ditch. The name of the station was drawn from the river a few miles to the north. Congress had allotted $5,000 for the tower, keeper's quarters and illuminating apparatus. That same year, the government issued a proposal for the erection of the lighthouse station. As more shipping traversed the bay, a lighthouse provided protection from the route from the Thimble Shoal Lightship and Old Point Comfort Lighthouse to the south and York Spit Lightship and the New Point Comfort Lighthouse due north. Breach Bar lay south of Back River Lighthouse. Nearby shoals victimized maritime traffic, such as the schooner the *President*, which ran aground at the mouth of the Back River in 1815, and the schooner *Rapid*, which ran ashore at the same location fifteen years later.[74]

In 1829, Winslow Lewis built the Back River Lighthouse. It was one of his more successful construction projects. *Library of Congress.*

In the spring of 1829, Moses Myers, a merchant and the collector of customs for Norfolk, issued specifications for the facility. Myers's supervisor was Stephen Pleasanton, the fifth auditor of the Treasury Department. The latter had no nautical experience and had numerous other duties in addition to overseeing navigational aids. For these reasons, Pleasanton came to depend on entrepreneur and mariner Winslow Lewis. A fellow New Englander and associate of Pleasanton, Lewis was an experienced merchant mariner, but he was not an engineer. Nevertheless, by the time of the construction of the Back River Lighthouse, he was the premier lighthouse advisor and contractor in the United States.[75]

Myers's request for the lighthouse bid noted: "Separate proposals will be received for fitting up the said Light House, within one month after it shall be built, with patent lamps and reflectors, fitted with clock work to cause the same to revolve....In the same manner as the light houses have been fitted up by Mr. Winslow Lewis—the whole to be approved by the superintendent." Moses required the proposals to be submitted by July 10; the aforementioned Lewis of Boston not surprisingly submitted the winning bid. The reference to Lewis and "Boston glass" in the Back River proposal were indicators of his favored position with the lighthouse establishment.[76]

Pleasanton prided himself on returning funds to the treasury at a time when European lighthouse services surpassed those in the United States in proficiency and in willingly embracing innovations. In short, Pleasanton sacrificed safety to save money. Ultimately, the Back River station cost $4,550.04, so he carried a surplus back to the treasury of $439.96. Before placing the winning bid of $3,500 for Back River Lighthouse and $750 for the lamps, Lewis had already won government contracts to supply the American lighthouse with whale oil and his patented lamps. The lamp system included in the Back River specifications was an amalgam of three European innovations, including those of Argand.[77]

Despite Winslow Lewis's enviable position, many of his contemporaries and later historians disparaged his contributions. In his lifetime, he was openly criticized by Isaiah William Penn Lewis, a nephew and business rival, the publishers of the *American Coast Pilot*, army engineers and naval officers. At the close of his career, a sweeping lighthouse inspection board remarked on the contractor's lack of engineering background and Lewis's poor construction techniques and lack of appreciation for how important these navigation aids were to the young nation.[78]

More specifically for the Back River Lighthouse, it is not clear whether Lewis supervised the daily construction of the station or subcontracted the project to other builders. The contract for Back River Lighthouse specified a whitewashed thirty-foot-tall tower with three windows and a three-foot-thick base tapering to twenty inches at its black top. Iron circular stairs led to a ladder below the octagonal lantern room with double-glazed sashes. The white lighthouse was contrasted against a black pointed dome with astragals topped with a copper lightning rod.[79]

Before starting construction, Winslow Lewis assumed the station was to be near the mouth of the Back River, not three miles to the south. Therefore, he anticipated landing building materials at the river's opening. He requested an adjustment to the site, but that request was not granted, and he had to transport the materials on a small boat. Other requirements for the station included the keeper's quarters, a stone-lined well (there was also a cistern), a footbridge to the tower, an outhouse and a kitchen. The cooking area was to be twelve by fourteen feet, with windows, an oven and a fireplace equipped with trammels and hooks.

From the beginning, Back River Lighthouse was strongly linked to the adjacent community of Fox Hill. William Jett, the site's first and longest-serving keeper, hailed from Northumberland County, but most of the caretakers were from Elizabeth City County: Robert T. Wallace, Reverend William N. Thornton, Elijah Wallace, James F. Hawkins, Richard F. Johnson and J.D. Johnson. Thornton and Southey Parker were Black keepers who served after the Civil War. The Wallaces and Johnsons were part of the kith of Fox Hill. The majority of the close-knit populace worked as watermen and farmers.[80]

The first steamer service from Baltimore to Norfolk was started in 1817, and it took about twenty-four hours to complete the trek. Just before the Civil War, that leg took half that time and included links to the nation's capital. Despite the presence of the lighthouse, in the 1840s, there was a series of nearby mishaps, such as the losses of the sloop *Hector* in 1842, the schooner *Mary Eliza* a year later and the *Norfolk*, which capsized off Back River on the night of October 13, 1845. It is supposed all on board perished on the *Norfolk*.[81]

In the summer of 1851, inspectors surveyed the Back River station as part of a national effort to improve the construction, illumination and location of the American light stations. This effort included examinations by naval officers and army engineers. Among the group that visited Back River was Lieutenant Colonel René E. De Russy. His review at Back River determined the light functioned and the tower was moderately clean but was in need of major repairs. There were issues involving the "air-fly" and revolutions of the light. The whitewashed tower, made of good brick, leaked. The ten lamps with thirteen-inch reflectors were well trimmed, and the lamps consumed about three quarts of oil a night. As per standard procedure, the logs indicated that the light was checked at 10:00 p.m. and 2:00 a.m. each night. The keeper's quarters were in "very good order," and there was a garden. The pipes to the cistern were in poor condition. Prior inspections had been made, but no repairs had been completed. More pressing than the need for maintenance was the threat of erosion. Immediately after the light's completion, the surrounding land began to erode into the bay, and continued efforts were made to save the tower.[82]

As for the light's personnel, Keeper William Jett, who had already served at the station for twenty-two years, was sick, so the inspectors met with Jett's son. It was not clear if Jett lived in the keeper's quarters and was so sick he was unable to see the inspectors or if he was sick at another location. Nevertheless, Keeper Jett unofficially enrolled an enslaved assistant described as a "negro man." The examiners observed that the man "has been engaged in light-keeping since his boyhood." The 1850 slave schedule for Elizabeth City County indicated that Jett enslaved five people. Two of the men were eighteen and twenty-five years old.[83]

In 1855, the installation received a revolving machine and reflecting illuminating apparatus that improved the light. The station featured six twenty-one-inch parabolic reflectors and six fountain lamps that could be seen at a distance of fourteen miles in clear weather. At the end of the decade, Major Hartman Bache of the Light House Board announced that Back River Lighthouse would be temporarily extinguished for unspecified repairs. A newspaper article in the *Daily Dispatch* penned by "Percussion" in Norfolk warned mariners to be extra careful while the light was extinguished, as there "is quite a shoal making out there, and this is considered about the worst post of the Bay."[84]

On April 17, 1861, Virginia departed from the Union to join the Confederacy. Many local white men enlisted in the secessionist cause. This sea change placed Keeper James Hawkins and his family in danger. Six miles due south of the lighthouse, Union troops still held Forts Monroe and Calhoun (later Wool). From that location in early May, Colonel Justin Dimmock reported to Flag Officer Garrett J. Pendergast that as "soon as the weather is favorable I will order the *Yankee* and first cutter of this ship to accompany Colonel De Russy to reconnoiter from here to Back River Light." Imagine De Russy's pensive thoughts: he had applied his skills as an engineer to improve the function of the light and secure it from storms. Now, he turned to his training as a soldier to protect Back River Lighthouse from marauders.[85]

A foray conducted in the summer reported "that Back River light was not burning." Among all this turmoil, Keeper Hawkins; his wife, Mary; and their six children waited. Unfortunately for the Hawkins family, the contingent that soon arrived at Back River was not his replacements or protectors. In September, Lieutenant John A. Dickson, commanding elements of the Burke Rifles and Buncombe Rifles of the First (Bethel) North Carolina Infantry, departed the Confederate defenses near Poquoson at dusk and journeyed south to the lighthouse in rowboats. There, the Confederates meet with sympathizers, who pointed to the station. This need for directions at night may have been an indicator that the light was not functioning or that the Confederates took a land route to the station.[86]

The North Carolinians surrounded the station. Hawkins offered no resistance. The raiders then "totally demolished" the lamps and buildings. Southern newspapers reported that the keeper's family was "treated with the utmost kindness and consideration." In contrast, Hawkins did not fare so well. He was branded a "southern traitor and Lincoln officer holder" by the *Charleston Courier*. The Confederates took the keeper to Yorktown and later released him. The Hawkins family survived their ordeal and remained in the area as farmers.[87]

Despite the Rebel incursion, the station was not dark for long. Union troops quickly reasserted control of the lower Virginia Peninsula. By April 1862, the Light House Board had anchored a lightship off the station. The following year, crews repaired the station. William H. Abdell and J.D. Johnson served as keepers during the war. To maintain control of the lighthouse, the federals erected a guardhouse. In 1863, Blunt's *American Coast Pilot* announced, "The light-house on Back River Point contains a revolving light elevated 35 feet above the level of the sea, and serves as a guide for vessels bound in the river, as well as to assist vessels bound up the bay." After the war, although the station functioned, it needed major repairs. Crews refitted the lighthouse door with hinges and locks, the tower and woodwork received two coats of whitewash, the windows were reglazed, the guard shack became an outbuilding and more riprap was added to the base of the tower.[88]

One of the more interesting postwar visitors to the station was bare-knuckle boxer Samuel Collyer (born Walter Jamieson). During the Civil War, Collyer earned the Congressional Medal of Honor for his heroics at Fort Harrison. The pugilist made Fort Monroe his training base for a forthcoming contest, but his morning runs took him to Back River Lighthouse. At that time, beachcombers walked regularly from Old Point Comfort to Back River.[89]

In 1870, when Reverend William N. Thornton assumed duties as the light's keeper, it was just one more aspect of his fascinating life. Thornton spent about half of his existence in slavery, leasing his skills as a carpenter to others. His days in servitude ended when, in the early months of the Civil War, federal troops in Hampton created a haven where countless bondsmen gained their freedom. From then on, Thornton shared the Gospel and assumed a leadership role in Hampton's growing Black community. He traveled to Boston for his ordination and to raise funds for ministry. In Middleton, Connecticut, Thornton and another formerly enslaved person from Hampton were slated to give what the newspaper the *Constitution* called "a contraband talk." The first lecturer "gave an interesting narrative of his life as a slave." Thornton was scheduled to address the membership the following night and was described as "an excellent speaker." Returning to Hampton, he later led the Zion Baptist Church, a congregation that continues to thrive.[90]

With the establishment of the Hampton Normal and Agricultural Institute (now Hampton University) in 1868, Thornton ministered at the school and continued his own education. In 1874, teacher Mary F. Armstrong recalled the pastor "struggling all by himself with the formidable outworks of an old Greek grammar in the fond hope of being able, some day to read his Testament in the original." The *Southern Workman*, issued by the institute, repeated this same vignette in Thornton's obituary. His journeys to the school were not just for his own edification. Twice in the 1870s, governors named Thornton as one of the school's "curators of the land script fund." After his tour as a keeper, his efforts to help others continued for the rest of his life.[91]

During his tenure as keeper (1870–77), he earned $540 as an annual salary to underpin his preaching. He headed a household that included his wife, Ellen, and eight children, but it is not clear if everyone lived with the pastor at the Back River Lighthouse. All told, there were seven adults in the Thornton household who may have executed the keeper's duties. Following his term at Back River, Thornton continued as the spiritual leader of Zion Baptist until 1889. When the nonagenarian died, hundreds of mourners marked his passing. The local *Daily Press* noted he "was a highly respected colored minister, and while not actively engaged he has continued as pastor emeritus of the church."[92]

Following Thornton, another formerly enslaved person, Southey Parker, assumed the duties as the head keeper of Back River Light. Parker may have served in the Union navy during the war. This expertise would transfer smoothly to lighthouse duties. He polished the skills he needed as the first assistant keeper at the important Thimble Shoal Lighthouse. Records from the U.S. Freedman's Bank indicated that Parker sported whiskers and was born on the Eastern Shore, but he grew up in Hampton and was employed by the light house service. When Parker was promoted to keeper at Back River, he resided at the house with his wife, Sarah, a nephew and an adopted child.[93]

In 1878, with the waters of the bay eager to consume the lighthouse, crews positioned one hundred cubic yards of stone along the base of the tower. Three years later, screens were used to keep the sand in place. Also, at this time, the kitchen received a new floor. In the summer of 1885, district engineer Major Jared A. Smith supervised the examination of the Back River Lighthouse and other lights in the area. A native of Maine, an 1862 graduate of the United States Military Academy and a Civil War veteran, Smith spent much of his career in lighthouse construction and harbor and channel surveys. Smith's party took photographs of the stations; the one of Back River may have included Keeper Southey Parker. The isolated setting included a whitewashed house with three outbuildings. A few trees provided shade for the two-storied keeper's house. An undulating catwalk connected the front porch to the tower. By 1888, another 450 cubic yards of stone had been added.[94]

After the Civil War, the Back River Lighthouse served several federal agencies in an array of purposes. The surveyors on board the U.S. Coast Survey (later U.S. Coast and Geodetic Survey) vessel the *Matchless* used the tower's location to create accurate charts. In the summer of 1884, Commander Charles D. Sigsbee, the skipper of the practice ship *Dale*, plotted a coastline cruise so naval cadets (midshipmen) could sketch the shore "from

In the summer of 1885, Major Jared A. Smith took a series of lighthouse images in the district, including several at Back River Lighthouse. The catwalk to the tower and its keeper's quarters were under constant threat of beach erosion. *The Mariners' Museum.*

Fort Monroe to Back River light." Sigsbee later commanded the ill-fated USS *Maine* when the warship was sunk dramatically in the Havana Harbor and triggered the Spanish American War.[95]

At the beginning of the century, the Back River Lighthouse's fourth-order lens sent a fixed, white signal that flashed every ninety seconds. The focal point was thirty-three feet, and it could be seen eleven nautical miles away. The following year, the Crisfield-bound schooner the *Thomas B. Schall*, transporting a cargo of fish oil, "went aground near Back river [*sic*] lighthouse," according to the *Daily Press*. Captain Herbert Connor on the tug *Imperial* was unable to free the schooner. Twice, Herbert's efforts resulted in a broken seven-inch hawser. A few days later, however, the crew managed to free the vessel after twelve hours of hard labor and proceeded to Maryland.[96]

In the fall of 1903, concern about erosion sparked a major undertaking. A working party from the USLHT *Thistle* were erecting a bulkhead to protect

This close-up image of the Back River station may include Southey Parker, principal keeper. *Photograph by Jared A. Smith; The Mariners' Museum.*

the keeper's quarters when a storm struck. The waves displaced riprap around the tower, washed away the protective breakwater wall and drove the pile driver and the sixty-foot tender ashore. Fortunately, the already-present crew worked for three days to save the quarters, installed a new walkway to the lighthouse and added more than four hundred feet of protective wall to the property. After the timber for the wall and other building materials were offloaded from the damaged tender, the *Thistle* was rescued from the beach.

The warmer season marked the arrival of the watermen's camps in anticipation of the return of migratory schools of fish that gathered in the estuary. From these bases, the watermen drove poles into the shallows to create a framework for their pound nets. In 1887, the federal government estimated there were one hundred pound nets from Old Point Comfort to Back River employing four hundred watermen. The seasonal catch along the lighthouse's waterfront included mackerel, shad, pompano, herring and occasionally sturgeon. On a spring evening in 1908, while off Back River Lighthouse, the steamer *Washington* journeyed up the bay surrounded by millions of fish that were thought to be herring (possibly menhaden) for at least an hour. Later that spring, watermen spotted two large whales off the lighthouse and, according to the *Daily Press*, "were as happy as the one which swallowed Jonah."[97]

In the fall of 1904, tragedy struck the lighthouse. Keeper Robert T. Wallace, according to the *Richmond Times Dispatch*, "dropped dead in the lighthouse tower after lighting his lamps for the night." Elijah Wallace, the keeper's son, filled in for a fortnight. That Elijah Wallace could substitute for his father was a good indication that family members often assisted with lighthouse duties. Keeper James Llewellyn, formerly of the Newport News Middle Ground Lighthouse, became the permanent replacement.[98]

During Llewellyn's tenure, a frightening scenario illustrated the importance of experienced keepers. When brothers Perry and Wilbur Miller of Mathews County headed home in a motor launch, the bottom fell out of the craft, and the men grabbed their life preservers. The pair attempted to remain together as they headed for shore but became separated. Perry washed ashore just south of the Back River Lighthouse in the middle of the night. Shortly thereafter, Keeper Llewellyn and Wilbur Miller launched a boat to find the missing brother. The rescuers found the exhausted survivor nearly unconscious two miles north of the station. Perry was well enough to travel to an uncle's home in Hampton, but Wilbur was too ill and was thought to be suffering from pneumonia. He remained in the care of the keeper. In contrast the rescue, during the summer of 1914, Keeper Llewellyn's daughter was married at the lighthouse in an afternoon ceremony witnessed by a handful of family members and friends. Such were the benefits of being a lighthouse keeper at such an idyllic location.[99]

Other developments in the area included the construction of the Grandview Hotel. A pavilion and amusements such as dancing accented the resort. Like the lighthouse itself, the original site of the hotel is underwater, but the popular establishment gave Back River Lighthouse another name: the Grandview Light. Another storm struck in 1915, and Llewellyn reported, according to the *Evening Sun*, the "the bulkheads about the base of the station and a cement walk leading from the keeper's quarters to the lighthouse washed away." That same year, crews automated the lighthouse. At the price of $4,298, acetylene gas replaced the oil wick lamps as the light's source of illumination. This was one of the earliest stations with this innovative feature. The keeper's house was disassembled and became the new home of the Smith family in Fox Hill. Richard F. Johnson, the station's last resident light keeper, continued in his caretaker status for another twenty years. During World War I, the U.S. Army's coastal artillery journal reported that "Bug Light" (the Thimble Shoal Lighthouse) and the Back River Lighthouse were used as observation posts and continued to be locales for cavalry training, despite the complaints about the sand fleas.[100]

The selection of gas, even though electricity had been introduced to the peninsula, was a logical choice—although there were sometimes problems with this fuel source. Given the remote location, the station would have required its own generator. At that time, many generators ran on coal. This would have required tons of fuel and a heaver to regularly feed the furnace. So, in essence, the full-time coal heaver would have replaced the light keeper. Gas-powered lights did not require daily human contact.[101]

With the passing of the excitement of the Roaring Twenties, the nation slipped into the Great Depression. Still, the lighthouse and beach attracted visitors. On the morning of September 11, 1931, Dr. Elisha Kent Kane III and his young wife, Jenny Graham Kane, journeyed to the beach. The couple was visiting Jenny Kane's family. Kane was a professor of romance languages at the University of Tennessee and a member of an eminent family in Kane, Pennsylvania (named in honor of the professor's grandfather). Kane's relatives had distinguished themselves in medicine, politics and military service.[102]

While at the lighthouse's ripraps, Jenny Kane fell or dove into the water and was not able to recover and appeared unconscious. Her husband claimed he went to her rescue. Professor Kane then rushed his wife to Dixie Hospital.

Percy Budlong traveled the Chesapeake Bay and elsewhere and maintained photographic journals of his adventures. *Photograph by Percy Budlong; The Mariners' Museum.*

The attending medical staff was not able to revive her. The professor and her family buried her remains in the St. John's Episcopal Church cemetery in Hampton. The first certificate of death documented that the thirty-three-year-old woman died as the result of an "accidental drowning" at "Grand View." All along, the professor remained at the home of his in-laws. Shortly thereafter, there was a twist in the story.[103]

The Graham family later convinced the Hampton coroner that the professor had murdered Jenny. Hampton's sheriff interviewed watermen who were clamming nearby at the time of the tragedy. Based in part on their remarks, authorities arrested the widower and held him without bond. Ironically, the Hampton Jail is not far from St. John's Church, and it was falsely reported that Kane could view his wife's grave site from his barred window. Authorities ultimately allowed Kane to post bail to prepare for his murder trial. Both families aligned the best legal teams available. The Graham family even hired additional assistance from the commonwealth's attorney. Dr. Elisha K. Kane II traveled from Pennsylvania to support his son.[104]

Jenny G. Kane's headstone in St. John's Church Cemetery in Hampton, Virginia. The translation from Dante's *Divine Comedy* reads, "There is no greater sorrow than to recall in misery the time when we were happy." *Author's collection.*

The murder trial had all the components of a film noir classic. A handsome professor of romance languages from a major southern university was accused of killing his attractive wife. Adding to the richness of the drama were the defendant's relatives—the fascinating Kane family—the scene of the isolated lighthouse and letters that linked the scholar to "another woman." In Kane's defense, physicians, colleagues and former students offered their support for the professor. This set the stage for what the *Washington Herald* summarized as the "charging of Prof. Kane with deliberately drowning his wife off lonely Back River Light."[105]

Along with the *Washington Herald*, a dozen other newspapers sent journalists to the trial. Judge C. Vernon Spratley allowed reporters a central location in the court, and additional telecommunications lines were established at the town's police headquarters. Press coverage of the trial included images of the lighthouse with a spot marking the location of Jenny's death. As the case went to the jury, reporter George E. Travis of the local evening paper the *Times-Herald* quipped that crowds packed the courtroom "to witness the final scene in the greatest show the Lower Peninsula city has offered in a decade." In that same spirit, the *Times-Herald* also announced: "Typical Holiday Crowd Sees Final Kane Court Scene." And through it all, the lighthouse served not as a beacon but as reference point for witnesses and experts describing the events involving the murder trial *Commonwealth of Virginia v. Elisha Kent Kane.*[106]

Above: A postcard of the cemetery surrounding St. John's Church of Hampton. It holds the graves of at least three lighthouse keepers and Jenny Kane. *Author's collection.*

Left: The sensational headlines of 1931 involving the Kane murder trial in Hampton. *Virginiana Collection, Hampton Public Library.*

Keeper R.F. Johnson, according to the *Daily Press*, "gave a technical discussion of the depths of the water around the lighthouse, stating that at low tide, the water was about three feet deep in front of the light and a little deeper on the south side. The tide rises and falls about three feet. There are no holes around the lighthouse, and on a calm day, there is practically no current." Bearing in mind that the keeper no longer resided at the station, the Kanes were also alone. In October, civil engineer and city manager Jefferson Chambers had surveyed the site, took soundings and also later testified as an expert witness.[107]

A black-and-white crime scene photograph taken in the fall of 1931 showed two tiny figures just below the horizon that aligned to the extended footbridge that led to the deserted tower. Automobile tire impressions appear as if they are going to bisect the horizon line but curve along the secluded shore as the land bends to greet the Back River in the distance. The vastness of the shoreline and sky, along with the anonymity of the distant figures, reminds one of the aura of isolation seen in *Nighthawks* (1942), painted by Edward Hopper, and in the film noir movies that were so popular at the same time.

Watermen who were clamming at a distance at the time of Jenny's death gave conflicting testimony about the intonation of the voices and movements of the professor and his wife. The lighthouse continued as the key geographic reference point for the trial. For example: waterman J.F. Holloway testified that while clamming about a half to three-quarters of a mile offshore, he heard screaming and saw two people "fifteen to twenty yards" north of the lighthouse interacting in "pocket-deep" water. At first, the screams seemed playful, but their tone changed to a more distressful pitch. He remarked it was "down tide" and around 10:30 a.m. based on the passing of a little steamer from Norfolk heading to Mathews County. When asked to give his bearings in relation to the tower, he claimed, "I would say around east northeast." And he also stated that the Kanes' car was "just below [south of] the Light a little piece."[108]

About one hundred witnesses, experts, colleagues and family members testified. After the parade of humanity made its way to and from the stand, the jury deliberated for almost four hours. The white male jurists found Kane not guilty, and the courtroom erupted in approval. The legal ordeal for the professor that began in September ended in December. The stigma involving the accusation of murder, however, remained with Kane. In due course, the professor remarried and raised a family.[109]

Stormy weather followed the turmoil in the courts. In August 1933, the Chesapeake-Potomac hurricane rumbled through southeastern Virginia.

The crime scene photograph taken in the fall of 1931 for the murder trial of Elisha K. Kane III. *Virginiana Collection, Hampton Public Library.*

The category-four storm brought century-high flooding of five to ten feet and took forty-seven lives. The tempest battered the little lighthouse and was one of a series of gales that eroded the beach. The lighthouse itself went dark in 1936, when the lighthouse service closed the station amid the Great Depression. The beach remained popular, and snapshots with the lighthouse as part of the coastal essence were a must. However, without a caretaker, the lighthouse fell victim to vandals. As the years passed, a rupture appeared at the base of the structure that expanded with each passing year. Invariably, the gap united with the opening of the doorframe.[110]

The weather-worn, whitewashed exterior gave way to reveal red brick walls. On the eve of America's entry into World War II, an article in the *Daily Press* recalled when "the old foundations and remnants of a wooden-pile bulkhead that retained the house's foundation from the shifting sands and time long after the dwelling and outhouses were removed." The article closed by referencing the death of Jenny Kane "just a few yards from the sea-slimed rip-rap stones of the beacon's isle."[111]

Back River Lighthouse after the coast guard no longer maintained the station. The tower collapsed in the fall of 1956, during Hurricane Flossy. *The Mariners' Museum.*

All the while, the little lighthouse remained the backdrop of countless church outings, adventures, lovers' strolls and beach parties. Hamptonian Diane "Nikki" Nickerson Tingen recalled family walks along the Grandview Beach. The highlight of the day came when her father cooked hotdogs skewered on coat hanger wires over an open fire pit. Foxhillan Robert C.

The author holding a broken brick from the Back River Lighthouse near the remains of the catwalk. Beachcombers will often find bricks from the tower after storms. *Author's collection.*

Deal remembered scaling to the top of the lighthouse on the interior rusty stairs. The danger of this undertaking occurred to Deal only after decades of reflection. He also recalled the winds from southern storms that pushed up the bay relocated clams among the riprap and along the shore. Locals like him then easily harvested the shellfish between the huge rocks when the storm passed. The sunbathers came to the shoreline, and the lighthouse accented this perfect vista. One Fourth of July shortly after World War II, the *Daily Press* reported, "The beach from Bay Shore [a segregated Black resort] all the way up to the Grand View lighthouse resembled the popular conception of New York's Coney Island."[112]

Meanwhile, the tower weakened with each raging gale. Hurricane Flossy, a dissipated storm that moved from the Gulf Coast into the Mid-Atlantic region, flooded the communities near Grandview, and on September 26, 1956, it pulled the abandoned tower into the Chesapeake Bay. As the years passed, all that remained visible were massive blocks of gray rubble.[113]

In the summer of 1972, the City of Hampton opened Grandview Park Beach (now Natural Nature Preserve), which included two and a half miles of beachfront within a 640-acre nature preserve. The spirit of the lighthouse

The remains of the catwalk of the Back River Lighthouse in 2020, with the light's protective riprap in the background. *Author's collection.*

remains in the community. The entrance to Fox Hill is marked with a colorful sign featuring the structure. Lighthouses—and not just those purchased at lawn and garden shops—are part of yard decorations along Beach Road. A few of them are elaborate pieces of folk art. Certainly, all the lawn art and signage are nods to the little beacon.[114]

4

DEEP WATER SHOAL

Watermen's Friend, 1855

Virginia water traffic from Richmond exported tobacco and grains to domestic and international ports. By the mid-nineteenth century, large vessels, such as the bark *Bachelor* bound for Ireland, ran afoul of the James River shoals. Fortunately, the forgiving, soft bottom released vessels such as *Bachelor* during high tide. When the steamship *Roanoke* grounded, the purser had to journey to Norfolk to hire another vessel to free the steamer. The *Norfolk Argus* originally reported the "night is represented as being extremely dark at the time of the grounding." By the 1850s, newspapers such as the *Daily Republic* mentioned the need for stations on this section of the river.[115]

The government's proposal to correct this hazard called for three similarly built stations about fifteen miles apart. The bids closed in early September 1853, and the potential contractors had four months to finish the stations once the government awarded the contract. Each structure was to rest on five piles with cross braces. British engineer Alexander Mitchell patented this method of pile construction. Later, wooden threaded poles or massive iron augurs screwed into a riverbed were known as screwpile lighthouses. Sometimes, holes were pneumatically driven into the bed, and the supports were inserted in the space. Regardless of the method, lights of this design were called screwpile lighthouses in the United States. The U.S. Lighthouse Service built dozens of these modest beacons along the Chesapeake Bay, and they came to symbolize the great estuary.[116]

The oxymoronically named Deep Water Shoal Lighthouse rested on an oyster shell bank opposite Lyon's Creek on the James River in two and a half feet of water above the high tide. The interesting name was derived from the shoal that suddenly yielded to a deep channel. The lighthouse itself was a one-story structure made of lapstrake weatherboarding with a nine-foot-tall ceiling, and it included a kitchen, a sitting room and storerooms. The facility also featured an iron water tank with gutters that served as a cistern, a cooking stove and a tin oil stand. There were four windows, three inside doors and two doors that opened to a railed gallery. The floor rested on a joist with tongue-and-groove boards. A wooden ladder led to the lantern room. The vertical astragals were six feet tall, and the glazed portions were about twenty-one inches wide and one-quarter inch thick. The roof was to be covered with boards with heavy cross tins. Rather than install a fifth-order Fresnel lens in the James River lighthouses, the board installed a large, press-glass masthead lens. Joseph H. Ransom served as the keeper, and Thomas Ransom was the assistant keeper.[117]

Not long after the lighthouse's opening, disaster struck. A storm followed by a cold spell froze the river and Hampton Roads. According to the U.S. Treasury's annual report from 1857, the building "suffered considerable damage from the ice and storms of the past winter." A temporary lightship and stopgap repairs allowed the station to function until an entirely new structure could be erected. In 1861, with the outbreak of the Civil War, the station again met disaster when Confederates darkened the light. When federal forces moved toward Richmond during the Peninsula Campaign, the structure once again fell into Unionist hands. However, when the federals withdrew down the peninsula, the light was no longer needed, and the lighting apparatuses were taken to Fort Monroe.[118]

European newspapers, such as the *Daily News* of London, warned that lights such as the one at Deep Water Shoal were "extinguished by the American rebels on the parts of the coast within their power." All told, the Confederates darkened more than 160 lighthouses. Efforts to replace the signal proved difficult. A federal naval report indicated the "rebels have been doing mischief at Deep Water light-house." To overcome these obstacles, before the end of the war, the board reestablished the light permanently with new fog bells. The *Light List* (1865) described its location as "on the shoal, starboard side of channel going up, above Mulberry Island Pt. and below Lyon's Creek."[119]

In early 1867, reports in the *Norfolk Virginian* warned of "solid ice" on the upper James River, and below, "Jamestown and the Deep Water Shoal Lighthouse were heavy fields of floating ice." As expected, the Light House

Board later announced a floe had crushed the reestablished Deep Water Lighthouse. The *Army and Navy Journal* echoed the dire news, proclaiming the light's "total destruction by ice." In addition, ice dragged supporting buoys off the station. Congress responded by appropriating $16,000 for the reconstruction effort—but not before craft such as the British brig *Goldfinder* became grounded and struck submerged vessels in the darkness.[120]

Later that same year, the USLHT *Tulip* reported to Fort Monroe from the district headquarters in Baltimore. The *Tulip* was the former USS *Isaac N. Seymour*, a gunboat in Hampton Roads that was later transferred to the lighthouse service. The steamer towed the schooner *Joseph Parker* to serve as a temporary lightship and transported the needed fixtures to get the station back online. The lead-colored schooner shone a fixed light that could be seen from a ten-mile distance. By January 1868, the permanent light was back in service and could be seen at a distance of nine miles.[121]

Around 1874, a young Santa A. Morse assumed control of the lighthouse.

The Virginian remained at the station for more than a decade. Morse and Assistant Keepers Thomas Hunt and Edward H. Brown were Black men. Morse's tenure ended abruptly in 1885 as part of a political purge. The anti-Readjuster paper the *Alexandria Gazette* announced that keepers at five stations, including "White Shoals and Deep Water Shoals, were informed today that they are suspended and that their successors will be appointed upon the recommendation of the Collector of Customs." The collector in Norfolk was also a political appointee and often controlled the appointment of keepers. Earlier, the *Alexandria Gazette* quoted Representative Harry Skinner of North Carolina, who reminded voters that when Republicans came to power, they "turned out every democratic [*sic*] incumbent of a lighthouse and replaced him with a republican." So, why should the Republicans have been "simply mystified" with the latest reshuffling when the Democrats returned to power? This wholesale turnover revolved around the election of Democratic president Cleveland and the decline of Mahone's influence in the Senate.[122]

This mosaic of a lighthouse at Buckroe Beach in Hampton is just one of hundreds of local business logos, lawn ornaments and flags that acknowledge the lighthouse culture of Tidewater, Virginia. *Author's collection.*

Starting in the early 1890s, range lights from Deep Water Shoal to Hog Island improved navigation on the channel. The additions were evidently needed but not always helpful, as evidenced when a Scotland-bound schooner was grounded between the island and the lighthouse. In 1907, the station itself was described as resting in two feet of water above Mulberry Point with a sixth-order lens that produced a fixed white light that could be seen at distance of eleven miles. This was a clear indicator of the hazard at the shoal.[123]

The new century brought a confusing number of changes to the station's staff. The lighthouse service removed Keeper J.J. Wilson from his post for sleeping and allowing the signal to go dark. James T. Parks became Wilson's replacement. A few years later, Swedish-born Olaf A. Olsen of Maryland replaced William S. Hudgins, who headed to Wolf Trap Lighthouse. Assistant Keeper Charles S. Hudgins succeeded Arthur L. Small following the latter's promotion to Hog Island Lighthouse. The last three men were from Mathews. Charles S. Hudgins soon transferred to Smith's Point. In 1907, Parks resigned. Despite the carousel of transfers, in 1909, Captain H.T. Mayo of the Light House Board praised Keeper Alexander P. Hurst for maintaining a well-ordered station. Another Mathews native, Hurst remained at the station at Deep Water until 1928, when he retired after thirty years of service.[124]

The waters surrounding Deep Water Shoal, like those that surrounded the other James River lights, at one time teamed with various oyster boats harvesting the succulent bivalve. Being from small, close-knit communities, these men happily exchanged tales. One yarn involved the killing of a daughter named Nell who married without her father's blessing. The angry patriarch then murdered his offspring. Nearby Nell's Creek supposedly bore her name. The spirit of Nell visited the watermen during the apex of the oyster business and would answer questions about catches and prime tonging locations by rapping on the boats' hulls. The spirit even rocked the boats when angered but did not appear to be a threat to the lighthouse.[125]

While the haunts of the river may have never gripped the light station, a bitter storm in early 1918 certainly rattled the building. Ice floes displaced

Olaf A. Olsen has been transferred from Deep Water Shoal light, Virginia, as assistant keeper of Hooper's Straits light.

Norwegian-American Olaf A. Olsen of Maryland was one of a relatively few foreign-born keepers in the district. *From the* Baltimore Sun, *August 24, 1902.*

Light keepers in the area often lent aid to pilots of seaplanes such as this U.S. Navy TS Wright XF 3W-1 during tests at Langley Field, 1927. *Wikimedia Commons.*

buoys, and authorities removed others to prevent their loss. Mariners were officially notified that the keepers at Deep Water Shoal, White Shoal and Point of Shoal were "authorized to leave," and the signals "may not be exhibited until their return." Simultaneously, during World War I, the U.S. Army assumed control of much of the area near Deep Water Shoal. The installations were originally known as Camp Abraham Eustis (later Fort Eustis and now Joint Base Langley-Eustis) and Camp Wallace. Coastal artillery was part of the original mission of the camp. At the close of the war, the *Lighthouse Service Bulletin* reported Assistant Keeper Robert H. Matthews "rescued from drowning four soldiers adrift in a sail boat during a storm in the vicinity of the light station."[126]

The activity on the river began to change. Two world wars brought maritime traffic to the fort. As ships became larger, there was a need to widen, deepen and better mark the channels and Mulberry Island Slough between Deep Water Shoal and White Shoal and still protect the interests of the oystermen concerned about public shellfish grounds in that part of the river.[127]

Principal Keeper George G. Johnson was one of the last keepers to serve at Deep Water Shoal. Under his leadership, in 1931, the station earned the efficiency star. Like many keepers, Johnson had time to ruminate on the changing events of the early twentieth century. One of those happenings was theaters operating on Sunday, even for charity. Johnson expressed his opposition to the practice in a letter to a council member. In short, the keeper declared, "I wish to say that I am thankful to God to know that the city of

Newport News has such men as yourself and others in it that will not permit an evil of this kind in your city on Sunday."[128]

During the Depression, the light and fog signal were discontinued, and the keeper briefly departed the station. The stations at Craney Island and Back River were taken out of service, never to be relit. In February 1936, there was a temporary light placed on the structure at Deep Water Shoals. The keeper returned, but on February 2, 1940, the station was once again discontinued. Another temporary light flashed a white signal every five seconds for one second—and it was then eclipsed for four seconds—at an elevation of thirty-one feet. For eight days, the regular characteristics of the light were restored. The temporary removal of keepers from Deep Water Shoal in the 1940s appears to have been done for safety reasons concerning ice floes, not as a cost-saving move during the Depression. The *Daily Press* informed mariners in February 1940 that ice "conditions in the James have greatly improved and the keeper personnel of the Deepwater [*sic*] Shoal Lighthouse have been returned to their stations."[129]

Deep Water Shoal Lighthouse. *The Mariners' Museum.*

World War II revitalized activity on the river, which blurred past the lighthouse. During live fire exercises, the lighthouse served as a boundary for the danger section, while the mouth of Skiff's Creek was the other marker. Red flags on safety towers also warned watermen and other mariners. When war erupted, the army established the Hampton Roads Port of Embarkation, and Fort Eustis was a key component.[130]

After the war, the coast guard requested the army run an electrical cable from Mulberry Point to the light. Meanwhile, hundreds of cargo and auxiliary naval ships found a home in the James River Reserve Fleet, popularly known as the Idle Fleet or Ghost Fleet. Into this setting, in 1953, maritime historian Alexander C. Brown journeyed up the river on the USCG *Narcissus* (WAGL-238) to Burwell's Bay to observe "the ghostly fleet [and] the James River's oldest surviving lighthouse." The Deep Water Shoal Lighthouse continued to be manned for just one more year before going dark. In 1966, the coast guard removed the station's framework and added a skeleton tower. The faded lighthouse was no longer guiding ships to rest among the ghost fleet, but the screwpile framework has remained.[131]

POINT OF SHOAL

Beacon of Burwell Bay, 1855

The ubiquitous James River oysters and sandy bottom formed the foundation for the Point of Shoal Lighthouse. Two feet of water covered the shoal at high tide, but it was exposed at half tide along the curve in the river along Burwell Bay. The Point of Shoal structure was identical in its origins and features to the Deep Water Shoal and Point of Shoal Lighthouses. In the fall of 1854, Thomas L. Kendall and John K. Floyd received appointments as keeper and assistant keeper, respectively. The pair started their duties the following year at this screwpile station just three and a half miles below Mulberry Island.[132]

The light withstood the fierce freeze of 1857, only to be threatened by the rebels during the Civil War. Keeper Kendall joined the Fifth Virginia Cavalry at Burwell Bay, despite being middle-aged. Federals removed much of the lighting fixtures to Fort Monroe. So, the light went dark until the U.S. forces needed the signal for operations against Richmond later in the conflict. The rejuvenated light came back online with new fog bells. After the war, Kendall returned as the keeper, and his wife, Susan Heath Kendall, worked briefly as the assistant keeper.[133]

The light's maintenance after the war included painting, the addition of a new lens for the Funck lamps, splicing the support beams, repairing the balustrades and ironwork and making new oars and boat falls. On a fall morning in 1869, the USLHT *William F. Martin* anchored off the light to deliver "Ten (10) glass chimneys and twenty four [*sic*] (24) lamp wicks." Before noon, the tender schooner was underway and changed spar buoys

COLLISION AND LOSS OF LIFE.—We learn from the Norfolk Beacon, that the steamship City of Richmond, Captain Mitchell, while on her passage from Richmond to that Port, about 9 1-2 o'clock Thursday night, off White Shoal, ran into the schr. Amazon, Capt. Jno. Moore, from Cherystone, with oats, bound to Richmond, sinking her immediately, and causing the death of Capt. Moore by drowning. The crew, two in number, were saved. The Amazon sunk in about five fathoms water.

The collision of the steamer *City of Richmond* and the schooner *Amazon* emphasized the need for lighthouses in that section of the James River. *From the Richmond Dispatch, March 12, 1855.*

along Lyon's Creek before proceeding to the Deep Water Shoal Lighthouse. There the tender brought a boat and fittings and two dozen lamp wicks. These supplies, however, could not overcome the wartime and harsh weather damage and poor building methods used in the construction of the Point of Shoal structure.[134]

Thomas Kendall departed Burwell Bay under tragic circumstances. An Englishman and the head keeper of Cape Charles squared off with shotguns. The duel resulted in the death of the keeper. Kendall then became the principal keeper. The deceased keeper's wife remained at the light as an assistant keeper. This arrangement was unusual but allowed a keeper who was experienced with the light to assist Kendall, who was the new arrival at a station quite different from the light at Point of Shoal. The female assistant keeper also remained employed when she needed it most. Back at Point of Shoal, shifts of keepers moved through the station until the Hatsells (Hatzells) of North Carolina assumed control of the station.[135]

The annual report from 1869 noted the structure was unsafe and facing another merciless winter season. The expectation rose that the building would be "carried away when ice breaks up." Therefore, beginning in the spring of 1871, crews began to rebuild the James River lighthouses. The work went smoothly until engineer Captain Peter C. Harris telegraphed headquarters in Baltimore "that the keeper was arrested and taken away on the charge of murder." Follow-up reports claimed Keeper Hatsell was innocent and that two workmen were serving temporarily as keepers. In addition, the crew members could testify that the keeper was not on shore the night of the murder.[136]

The residents of Surry County had made an unsubstantiated connection between the lighthouse work crews, the lightkeeper and a disturbing crime. On May 27, the murder of Littleberry Pittman, a well-respected resident living near Bacon's Castle, caused alarm. Apparently, around midnight, three white men in blackface and wearing federal army uniforms intruded on the property of the Pittman family. When the patriarch investigated the disturbance, one of the intruders blasted him with a shotgun. The armed trio then went to the house and threatened to kill Pittman's wife if she interfered with their search for valuables. A girl also witnessed the home invasion and escaped to tell the neighbors. A search led the pursuers to Rock Wharf on Burwell Bay, where the perpetrators escaped in a boat. A connection was made between the crime scene and the lighthouse personnel. The *Norfolk Virginian* reported "the impression in the neighborhood is that some of the party at the lighthouse must have committed the crime."[137]

Two weeks later, the investigation led detectives to bring Keeper William Hatsell to the justice at Surry Courthouse under the suspicion of murder. He was arrested. The keeper retained legal counsel, and after a "protracted investigation" and trial, he "was acquitted of the charge." The article in the *Norfolk Virginian* does not report what role the head keeper's wife, Assistant Keeper Rebecca Pigott Hatsell, played in the investigation. It is not clear if the detention of Hatsell was politically motivated and a ploy to intimidate the keeper. Given that the perpetrators wore federal uniforms and blackface, this may have been a weak effort to implicate Black soldiers in the U.S. Army who would have part of an attachment of troops during Reconstruction. This tension may have been a reason for the departure of both keepers the following year.[138]

The navigational concerns adjacent to the station justified the rebuilding efforts. A report to the secretary of war in 1882 noted the reef of Point of Shoal "is considered by the oldest pilots to be too hazardous to attempt to pass it in the night." The thirty-foot-deep channel elapses to a shoal abruptly, endangering vessels even in the daytime. The report recommended additional markers for the hazards. Four years later, during the earthquake of 1886, the keeper reported "he felt three distinct shocks of earthquake on August 31. The first was felt at 9:50 p.m., local time, and there was just about five minutes between shocks. The first was very heavy, the second was not so

THE LIGHTHOUSE-KEEPER.

This view of a keeper during the late 1800s reinforces the impression of isolation from the cares of the surrounding world. However, this was the era when political involvement of many keepers peaked. *Author's collection.*

heavy, and the third was very slight." This is fairly consistent with the report from Old Point Comfort, where the estimated time of the big quake was 9:55 p.m., and the quake from the epicenter in Charleston, South Carolina, was thought to have started at 9:51 p.m.[139]

In 1881, Peter F. Blount, a Black landowner from Isle of Wight County, was transferred from White Shoal to Point of Shoal, where he became the head keeper. He replaced William Washington. Blount then left the lighthouse position to become the postmaster of Smithfield. According to Professor James T. Moore, during this Readjuster era, "Postmasterships and clerkships were particularly prized." So, this move for Blount would have been a promotion. Blount held that position until 1885, when Democratic president Grover Cleveland moved into the White House. The Democrats then moved to free the postmaster's position for someone with their political

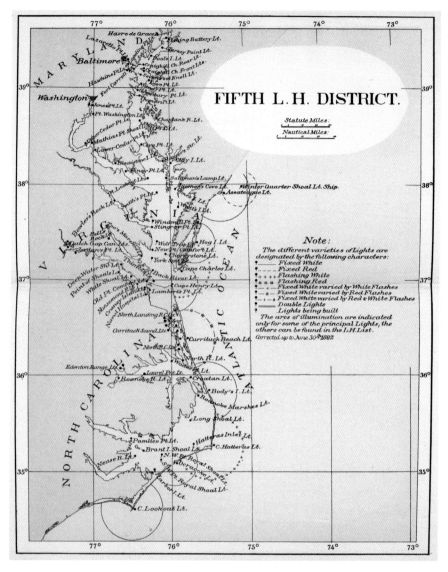

This map from the 1880s shows the Fifth District when it ranged from Maryland to northeastern North Carolina. As of 2023, the district stretches from New Jersey to North Carolina. *Library of Congress.*

affiliations. At the close of the decade, both Blount and Washington served as Republican delegates in the Second District.[140]

Guides on navigation at the beginning of the twentieth century described the White Shoal Lighthouse as a white hexagonal structure in about two feet of water resting on brown piles or supports. There were two red sections (331½ degrees to 350 degrees and from 179 degrees to 190½ degrees) on the sixth-order signal that flashed thirty-three feet above the water. For the white sector, the 270-candlepower light could be seen from a distance of eleven miles. For the two red sections, the power was 80 candlepower. The fog signal bell sounded one stroke followed by five seconds of silence and then another single stroke followed by two seconds of silence.[141]

The light on the northeast side of the channel eventually became obsolete, as the bight of Burwell Bay continued to shoal and engineers dredged a new channel two miles to the east. In 1932, the station was automated. The following year, the light was discontinued. The coast guard dismantled the lighthouse, but its iron foundation remains.[142]

6

WHITE SHOAL

Station on the Half Shell, 1855

B etween Pagan Creek and the James River emerged White Shoal. While the waterway is broad like the other rivers in Tidewater, Virginia, the S-shaped turns of the James River made navigation tricky. The shallows supported oyster beds, which were exposed at half-tide, and thus, the name "White Shoal" or "White Shoals" emerged. In 1855, the federal government spent $1,000 each for three lighthouses at Deep Water Shoal, Point of Shoal and White Shoal. The previous year, James H. Wilson accepted the position of principal keeper for $500 a year. Dempsey M. Crumpler became the assistant keeper for $300 per year.[143]

According the Treasury Report from 1856, the light beamed with a "large-sized press-glass masthead lens [that] was suspended in the lantern of each house" instead of a fifth-order Fresnel lens that might have otherwise served the station. The light endured the incredibly harsh winter of 1857, only to be extinguished by the rebels at the beginning of the Civil War. The station's change in fortune made the *Daily News* of London's list of "lights extinguished by American rebels." When the federal forces advanced up the Virginia Peninsula in 1862, the screwpile lighthouses were relit. When the campaign failed and the federals withdrew to Fort Monroe, the stations were once again extinguished. Later, as the federals gained more control of Virginia, beacons like the one at White Shoal were rekindled with new a fog bell and illuminating apparatus.[144]

The war ravaged the James River lighthouses and revealed flaws in their construction. In addition, the winter of 1867 greatly damaged the *Deep*

This four-story-tall mound of oyster shells in Hampton was part of the business empire of J.S. Darling and Sons. Watermen of the region harvested the shellfish to be processed in Hampton. The shells were then repurposed as aggregate for roads, walkways and oyster beds. The lighthouses on the James River guided the watermen. *Author's collection.*

Water Shoal Lighthouse (and those at White Shoal and Point of Shoal to a lesser extent). The annual report from 1869 claimed the structure "canted to the westward about one foot from the vertical at the top and the whole structure is in a very unsafe condition." The leadership at the district headquarters thought another rough winter would doom the station. Wooden pilings sleeved in iron were added to protect the station against the ice. By 1871, the new station was completed along the lines of Deep Water Shoal and featured a new boat and davits, clock, lens and Funck lamps.[145]

From 1880 to 1917, at least six Black keepers served at White Shoal Light: Peter F. Blount, Park(er) Charity, Edward H. Brown, Thomas Hunt, George Thomas and George W. Holloway. The appointments of most of these men revolved around the Readjuster movement in Virginia politics. Blount transferred to Point of Shoal and was replaced by Charity, who soon resigned. Assistant Keeper Brown drowned in the summer of 1885 while trying to retrieve a boat that had gone adrift. Thomas served almost a decade as the head keeper. Later, Keeper Holloway ran the lighthouse for many years. He was one of the last serving Black lighthouse keepers appointed during the Readjuster era.[146]

White Shoal Lighthouse. *The Mariners' Museum.*

In the spring of 1907, Head Keeper "Captain" Millard F. Simonsen was suddenly struck with paralysis but still managed to tend to the light. The next day, he was able to send out a distress signal. An excursion vessel responded to the sign. According to the *Daily Press*, the keeper was "in a pitiable condition when discovered by a launch party from Smithfield." Women from the excursion boat *Jack Wilson II* were among the rescuers who lent him aid. The keeper insisted that he remain at his station until a replacement arrived to properly attend the light. Simonsen was then transported home to Portsmouth for treatment. He did recover and return to his duties. The keeper's dedication attracted media attention from as far away as Saskatchewan in its *Leader-Post*. Simonsen later returned to his duties at White Shoal and retired after World War I.[147]

In the early twentieth century, the station rested in about four feet of water on the northern side of the main channel. Its sixth-order lens flashed a fixed white light. The beacon shone about thirty-three feet above sea level. By 1923, the white light was visible from eleven miles away, while the red light warning was visible from a distance of eight miles. The bell fog signal was struck every ten seconds. Like the other lights on the James River, the beacon protected the oyster boats, lumber and coal schooners, bay steamers and government traffic toward to the newly created Fort Eustis. The lighthouses of the river served as boundary markers for the oyster beds for both harvesting and planting seed oysters. The beds were so important to the economy that when plans were made to deepen and widen the channel, the changes had to be made to project the beds.[148]

The harsh freeze of 1918 created havoc among the region's navigational aids. Ice floes moved buoys and channel markers. Authorities even granted keepers permission to abandon their respective stations on the James River. The *Notice to Mariners* declared "keepers…have been authorized to leave and the lights may not be exhibited until their return." Once the bitter weather moved on in the spring, the Old Dominion steamer *Brandon*, departing from Richmond, ran aground near the White Shoal Lighthouse. The steamer failed to clear the shoal, and about fifty passengers were transferred to the steamer *Pocahontas* to complete their journey to Norfolk.[149]

On a spring morning in 1931, Joseph E. Nettles, a *Daily Press* journalist, boated to the White Shoal Lighthouse in search of one of those human interest stories that so often featured lighthouse keepers. As he scaled the ladder to the quarters, he was surprised at the expansive station. He sought permission to approach as if he was boarding a vessel. Once on board, he found the head keeper, John R. Edwards, a fifty-year-old veteran of the lighthouse service. Nettles even referred to Edwards as a captain, a common practice to honor experienced keepers. The overall pristine state of affairs captured Nettles's attention. Edwards remarked that painting, cleaning and polishing kept him busy. He was even painting when Nettles approached the station.[150]

As the keeper was visibly isolated from human contact, the journalist inquired about Edwards's desire have a wife, family and home of his own. The keeper found the questions amusing and informed his guest that he had a home, wife and two children in Norfolk. And he enjoyed his monthly

Businesses and travelers of the Chesapeake Bay relied on a variety of sailing craft and steam-powered vessels. *Author's collection.*

White Shoal Lighthouse. *The Mariners' Museum.*

shore leave—or as Edwards put it, "I'm a bachelor twenty-two days each month and a married man the other eight." Edwards mused as he adjusted his pipe and returned to his painting and remarked that while it does get lonely, the water has an alluring fascination.[151]

Three years after this interview, the Light House Board automated the White Shoal Lighthouse by erecting a steel tower near the old station. Keeper Edwards served at Deep Water Shoal before he retired. In the 1970s, the remains of the old station collapsed and were removed. Sadly, by this time, the oyster industry was in sharp decline. It was not until the beginning of the twenty-first century that conservation and regulatory efforts began to revive this facet of the commonwealth's culture. In that same vein, developers built a replica screwpile lighthouse on the Pagan River that became part of the Smithfield Inn. An article in the *Daily Press* in 1988 made comparisons between the new undertaking and the White Shoal Lighthouse. Later promotions, however, claimed the inspiration for the current lighthouse is the Thomas Point Lighthouse in Maryland. Regardless of the source of the inspiration, the effort is certainly a nod to the importance of screwpile lighthouses to the region's culture.[152]

7

CRANEY ISLAND

In the Eye of the Storms, 1859

W hile the Chesapeake Bay introduces mariners to the calmer waters of Hampton Roads, the trip is not without its dangers. The Hampton and Craney Island Flats are to be avoided. Therefore, the U.S. Treasury positioned its first lightship off Willoughby Spit. Shortly thereafter, in 1820, because of rough conditions, authorities transferred the unstable lightship to the Craney Island Flats at the mouth of the Elizabeth River. This move created the nation's first permanent lightship station. John Pool(e) of Hampton won the contract to construct the lightship. It was a copper-fastened seventy-ton yawl with davits, a capstan and four berths. Cramped, expensive to maintain and unstable, these boats were improved through trial and error. Nevertheless, they were critical to local navigation until the mid-nineteenth century when screwpile lighthouses began to replace them.[153]

The word *lightship* is a misnomer. These vessels were first described using a variety of terms, such as *floating lights* and *light-boat*, before the later agreed-upon monikers of *lightship* and *light vessel* were used. The *Evening Post* referred to the station as the "Craney Island Light Vessel." In 1822, Edmund M. Blunt's *American Pilot* noted that a "vessel having a light at her mast-head has been placed at the extremity of Craney Island flats in 4½ fathoms of water." At least five different boats (C, Q, R, 21 and 23) served as the Craney Island Lightship. From Norfolk, vessels were rotated to make repairs and upgrades. Whatever their descriptor, lightships were often driven off station by storms, like the spring gale in 1831 that the drove Craney Island Light Vessel westward.[154]

The flats along Craney Island stalled the British advance on the island's defenses. The British intrusion into Hampton Roads spurred the need for coastal forts such as Fort Monroe. *Author's collection.*

The lightship took its name from Craney (sometimes Crany) Island, a crook of land that signaled to sailors the flats and bight on the Elizabeth River were opening to Hampton Roads. Sewell's Point and Craney Island narrowed the river channel to Norfolk and Portsmouth. The place's name was commonly linked with the herons misidentified as cranes that nested on the twelve-acre islet. During the War of 1812, American forces anchored their defenses of Norfolk on the island. Landing barges ran aground on the flats, thus throttling the British efforts and saving Norfolk.[155]

As the generations passed, the island served as a platform for a powder magazine, a quarantine station, a refugee camp and a fuel depot. In 1827, the French frigate *La Circe*, coming from Cuba, anchored off the island. One surgeon died and another became ill. About thirty-five crew members stricken with yellow fever were landed on the island to prevent contact with the towns. The quarantine anchorage near the island and Lambert Point protected local ports from the likes of yellow fever, cholera and smallpox. In early 1855, the sloop-of-war USS *Plymouth* returned from Japan as part of a historic venture led by Commodore Matthew C. Perry. Commander John Kelly anchored the sloop "below Craney Island Lightboat." According to the *New York Times*, the three-and-a-half-year "ground-breaking expedition to open trade doors into Japan" required the vessel to rest "in quarantine."[156]

For decades, Captain John Tee commanded the lightship. He earned $450 annually for his labors. Tee and his crew of three manned the ship during a revealing inspection. The examination noted the seventy-two-ton, thirty-four-foot-long (along the waterline) vessel was stabilized by a mushroom anchor. The fog bell could be heard five miles to the leeward. The station, however, was "in bad order." The "miserable" lantern that consumed 274 gallons of oil in six months was "too small." Commentary at the time that included the Virginia pilots observed "that the light at Craney island was so defective that a change of color was recommended on account of the difficulty of distinguishing it from the light of [other] vessels." Other issues concerned keeping lightships in place during violent weather, thus confusing mariners in a moment when the floating signal was needed most.[157]

During mid-January 1857, a horrific nor'easter ripped through the region. The blizzard toppled chimneys and froze birds, schooners and steamboats alike in an icy grip. Residents strolled across eight inches of ice from Norfolk to Portsmouth and even ventured across Hampton Roads. The *Norfolk Argus* reported, "Craney Island is distinctly seen five miles distant, surrounded by rugged banks, while the ice-bound vessels stand motionless as surf-beaten rocks." One of these frozen vessels may have been the Craney Island Lightship. Many passengers from the steamer the *Roanoke*, which was anchored a couple miles from the lightship station, walked on the ice to Norfolk. When the steamer *Virginia* reached Richmond from Norfolk, false rumors circulated through the *Daily Dispatch* that the "captain of the Craney Island Light Boat" had "drowned by breaking through the ice."[158]

In 1852, Captain James Hicks of the steamer the *Coffee* complained about the effectiveness of the lightship. Progressive thinkers, such Lieutenant Washington A. Bartlett of the U.S. Navy, pushed for the Craney Island operation to be upgraded to a lighthouse with a Fresnel lens. This innovation, developed by French physicist Augustin-Jean Fresnel, was the foremost advancement in lighthouse technology of the nineteenth century. Bartlett noted, "It was the pilots of Norfolk, and not of New York, who reported that the vessels which anchored in Craney Island channel created confusion by showing lights which were constantly being mistaken for Craney Island light." A few years earlier, Bartlett had been assigned to purchase lenses in Europe. Sadly, this assignment cost the lieutenant his commission. Claims were made regarding purchasing irregularities, and he was dismissed from the service.[159]

In 1859, the U.S. Light House Board constructed a fifty-two-foot-high facility at the western end of the Craney Island Flats in three feet of water. The screwpile octagonal structure was similar to the stations built along the lower James River four years earlier. In the fall, the *Alexandria Gazette* reported the "piles are already down and the frame braced, and a week or two more will find the light shining." The new fixed light with a Fresnel lens, located twenty yards from the lightship, was visible for twelve miles. The installation also featured a fog bell and horn. The lighthouse was scheduled to shine for the first time on November 15. It appears that George and Elizabeth Cross were the first keepers of the newly minted lighthouse.[160]

Fatefully, when the Civil War broke out in 1861, the station could not have been in a more precarious position. Even before Virginia left the

The Rip Rap Brewing Company of Norfolk has drawn on the once ubiquitous screwpile lighthouse for its logo. *Rip Rap Brewing Company.*

Union, secessionists grabbed gunpowder at the magazine on Craney Island and sunk lightships on the Elizabeth River to snag departing Union warships. The federals held fast to Forts Monroe and Calhoun (later Wool) and blockaded the roadstead. On the south side, much closer to the Craney Island, the Confederates damaged the Craney Island Lighthouse and moved into the Gosport Navy Yard, the customhouse in Norfolk and the Cape Henry Lighthouse. The Rebels then deployed artillery pieces on the island and at Sewell's Point. Occasionally, the batteries dueled with probing Union warships.[161]

The following year, on March 8, the ironclad CSS *Virginia* steamed from the Confederate-held Gosport up the river. Thomas O. Selfridge, an officer on the ill-fated USS *Cumberland*, recalled "the low hull [of the CSS *Virginia*] came in view abreast of Crany island light heading for the mouth of the Elizabeth river....All hands were called, the sails quickly furled, and the quick beat to 'quarters' aroused everyone." The ironclad sank the *Cumberland* and USS *Congress*, and the next day, it clashed with the Union ironclad USS *Monitor*. This was the first time that ironclad ships dueled in battle. Two months later, the Confederates evacuated Norfolk and Portsmouth.[162]

This compelled the crew of the *Virginia* to ground and then destroy their ship across from the lighthouse. The blast may have further damaged the station, as the lens had already been removed and the station ransacked during the first year of the war. Selfridge's mention of the lighthouse the following year is interesting. Selfridge wrote his article in 1893 and may have used old or contemporary charts for reference points, even though the lighthouse was in shambles. Or the remnants of the lighthouse may have been visible from Hampton Roads at the time of the battle.[163]

Federal authorities moved quickly to reestablish navigational aids. The stopgap effort started with positioning light vessels at Craney Island, Willoughby Spit and Back River. The Treasury Department described the island's lightship as "painted lead color, and having one light at her masthead. Thirty-three feet above the sea, has been placed at the extremity of Craney's Island Flats, in Elizabeth River, in 4½ fathoms [about 29 feet]." While the lighthouse was under construction, its keepers stayed on the island until crews finished the house. By 1863, the Light House Board reestablished the station on the west side of the Elizabeth River channel with a fifth-order lens with a light that was visible at a distance of thirteen nautical miles. The screwpile station featured a white, square wooden structure that was fifty-one feet tall with a brown roof. The fog signals included a bell and a horn.[164]

In the 1870s, the Fifth District's superintendents appointed numerous married couples as keepers. The men were the principal keepers, and the women served as assistants. Women keepers reached the highest number during this decade across Hampton Roads and the nation. During this span, two couples maintained the installation: Mary Jane (née Bell) and William P. Sturtevant, followed by Elisha and Phebe D. (née Williams) Richards. The biographies of the last two couples had some uncanny parallels. William P. Sturtevant was from North Carolina, and Mary Sturtevant was a native of Virginia. William served briefly as a first sergeant in the Third Virginia Infantry before being released due to asthma. The pair was married in 1842 and raised one dozen of their own children and two other adopted siblings. At the time they assumed responsibility of the lighthouse, it is not clear where the Sturtevant children resided. Unfortunately, the pair's tenure at the lighthouse was short. Following Mary's death in 1874, William returned to his former trade as a painter.[165]

Following the Sturtevants, the Richardses assumed the duties at the lighthouse. Elisha was born in New Jersey; Phebe hailed from Pennsylvania. Before the Civil War, the Sturtevant family lived a middle-class existence in Hancock, New York, with their two children, a male clerk and an Irish servant. William worked as a middle-class merchant. It appears the family hit on hard times, because by the time of the 1860 census, the family resided in Sioux City, Iowa. Phebe taught and William practiced law. Their economic decline may have been linked to the Panic of 1857. At any rate, their property holdings had greatly diminished to a little more than one hundred dollars.

A year after the Civil War began, William enlisted in the Twenty-Seventh New Jersey as a private and served nine months before he was discharged. By 1874, Elisha and Phebe were earning $540 and $420, respectively. The pair later served briefly as the keepers at Old Point Comfort on the north side of Hampton Roads. Their stint as light caretakers lasted about four years. It came to an end suddenly in 1879, with William's death from apoplexy—it's possible he died from a stroke. Phebe closed her life as a pensioner, living as the senior member of her daughter's family in Virginia.[166]

In 1880, the station received a new coat of paint, but the structural maintenance issues were far more troubling. A few years later, a report determined the "superstructure of this light-house is decayed. During every rain it leaks. The necessary lumber and mill-work for a new building were purchased, and its construction will soon be undertaken." In 1883, the crew of the USLHT *Jessamine* assisted with rebuilding the station. The new white structure was changed to a hexagonal shape that was rested on vertical piles. The black lantern section made the station thirty-four feet tall at the mean high-water mark with a fifth-order lens visible for eleven nautical miles. The station also featured davits for two boats, which allowed the keepers to perform lifesaving duties and commute to the island.[167]

In the spring of 1881, Haywood B. Pettigrew, a former first sergeant in the Second U.S. Colored Cavalry, assumed the duties as principal keeper, having transferred from Cape Henry. Pettigrew may have made the move so his wife, Amy W. Pettigrew, could assume the duties of an acting assistant. This may have been the only time a Black couple officially ran a lighthouse in Virginia. Haywood Pettigrew was one of many Black lighthouse keepers appointed during the Readjuster movement. This brief era saw Black and white political leaders in Virginia share power and federal government patronage. Professor Jane Dailey, in her study *Before Jim Crow: The Politics of Race in Postemancipation Virginia*, determined at that time, 27 percent of the commonwealth's employees in the Treasury Department were Black men. "And since Virginia was a coastal state, there were customs houses, lighthouses and lifesaving service to be staffed [by Black men]."[168]

Around 1905, a schooner snagged its anchor in the bight of Craney Island on a submerged chain that may have belonged to the CSS *Virginia*. Efforts to recover the chain and anchor failed. Two years later, another schooner, the *Mary Sanford*, found the ironclad's chain. The location was described later in the *Baltimore Sun* as "just inside Craney Island Light." The new efforts employed a derrick to recover the massive five-ton artifact for the 1907 Jamestown Exposition at Sewell's Point. The exposition marked the three hundredth anniversary of the first permanent English settlement in America.[169]

At the close of 1906, Keeper John Brown resigned after thirty-six years of service. Brown, unlike most men in the district, was a native New Englander and had arrived in the Old Dominion after the Civil War. Much of his service was in southeastern Virginia at the Willoughby Spit Lightship, Thimble Shoal Lighthouse and, finally, Craney Island Lighthouse. Keeper J. Filmore Hudgins of Mathews County became Brown's replacement. Hudgins was another stalwart of the district. He served at eight stations over thirty-seven years. Hudgins died in 1949 at the age of ninety-seven. German-born assistant keeper Charles W. Vette transferred to Craney Island, closer to his home in Portsmouth, in 1910. The following year, he retired. The *Baltimore*

Sun remarked, "Mr. Vette is a retired man-of-wars-man and musician and artist." One can imagine the muse-filled waters of Hampton Roads filling the old sailor's artistic soul.[170]

In 1910, Eastern Shore (Accomack and Northampton Counties) natives began to tend the light. James Hillary Quillen served briefly as an assistant keeper. Andrew Jackson Potts of Chincoteague worked as an assistant. Both men later returned to the Eastern Shore to care for the Cape Charles and Hog Island Lighthouses. Head Keeper Charles A. Sterling, a native of Accomack County, having served at Hog Island and Tangier Island, spent most of his distinguished career at Craney Island. In 1914, he relocated his family to the Norfolk area. Mustachioed, slight of build and of medium height, Sterling received more media coverage than any other keeper in the area.[171]

While Sterling was at Craney Island, Secretary of Commerce William C. Redfield praised the keeper "for recent meritorious conduct." Sterling rendered assistance to the drifting gasoline boat *Daisy*. He also assisted the sailing vessel *Mary Sen* when it went aground. In June 1915, a barge of freight cars broke from the towing tug *Henrico* during a storm and crashed against the iron framework of the lighthouse. The barges collided "with such force that the structure was loosened from its foundation [and] continued to pound against the station for nearly two hours before the tug could get control of it again," according to the *Evening Sun*. Sterling thought the structure would be wrecked as the calamity carried away a boat and its davits. The rocking motion compelled the keeper to clamp down the lens. Later, the USLHT *Ivy* rendered aid. The government concluded that neither the barge nor the tug was responsible for the more than $4,000 needed for the repairs.[172]

The transition from coal to diesel power for ships resulted in the slow conversion of Craney Island and its flats from a military outpost and quarantine station into an extensive fuel depot. The demand for space was so great that engineers bulkheaded the flats that connected the flats and the island to the mainland—although the location is still referred to as "Craney Island." The district headquarters also added additional riprap at the base of the station. Across the river, a greater transition was underway. Starting in World War I, the navy began to operate seaplanes at Sewell's Point. Eventually, the complex evolved into Naval Station Norfolk, the largest concentration of major warships in the world.[173]

Keeper Sterling took his own steps to support the war effort. Aside from contributing to the Red Cross, he cultivated peas, beans, turnips and cabbages in a victory garden on Craney Island from the seeds supplied to him by the first officer of the USLHT *Holly*. This was part of a national effort to have keepers provide for themselves. Some keepers even canned their own fish. Sterling also gathered driftwood and flotsam while on leave due to a shortage of coal. This last undertaking was certainly ironic, as Hampton Roads was one of the world's leading coal-exporting ports. Still, the Spanish flu pandemic, at that time, created numerous shortages, including that of coal. Sterling's multiple efforts were driven, in his own words, by a desire to "avenge the Hun that killed my nephew."[174]

Starting in 1918, the now-dubbed "Captain" Sterling and the assistant keepers completed a string of notable rescues. Sterling assisted a gasoline motorboat and a sailing vessel from drifting beyond the station. He also aided a couple in a disabled gasoline launch and, according to the *Lighthouse Service Bulletin*, "furnished them dry clothing, lodging, and food for one day and night." In that same spirit, Assistant Keeper John E. Stubbs rescued a trio of young men from drowning and provided them with dry clothes after their boat capsized. On March 19, 1922, Sterling assisted the disabled motorboat *Loretta* that drifted into the riprap protecting the lighthouse. For this act, Secretary of Commerce Herbert Hoover commended him for his "meritorious service." Two years later, Assistant Keeper James W. Stowe also saved two people from drowning.[175]

These trials prepared Sterling for what would be a spectacular rescue. On a pleasant evening in the summer of 1924, the excursion steamer *Gratitude* headed for the Elizabeth River. The vessel and its 288 passengers, including families associated with the Texas Company (later known as Texaco), were returning from a day trip to Jamestown Island. Along the Craney Island Flats, about four hundred yards from the island and five hundred yards northwest of the lighthouse, the ship struck a submerged scow. The impact hurled passengers into the sea, and the vessel took on water and quickly listed to starboard. Moments later, the ship went dark and signaled its distress with four sharp whistle blasts.[176]

Sterling leaped to action. He sounded a warning bell and notified the crew of the passenger steamer *Pennsylvania* of the ongoing disaster. The captain of that ship then headed to the scene and dispatched lifeboats. Sterling launched his own boat, and the *Virginian-Pilot* quoted a passenger who claimed the "first rescue boat to reach the wreck…was a lifeboat which Captain Sterling, keeper of the Craney Island lighthouse brought out." The paper also reported that "panic…gripped the excursionists." Subsequent newspaper reports attempted to downplay the passengers' sense of fear.[177]

When dawn broke, the *Gratitude* had listed in about four feet of water; the bow was slightly elevated as it rested on top of the sunken scow. The vessel

Gratitude Awash on Craney Island Flats

Stranded near Craney Island Light, Principal Keeper Charles A. Sterling earned his first silver lifesaving medal for saving the passengers of the SS *Gratitude*. *From the* Virginian-Pilot, *July 28, 1924.*

sank so quickly, there was no opportunity for fire to erupt. Sterling earned another official commendation "for heroic work" and later garnered a silver lifesaving medal. First awarded in 1874, the decoration acknowledged Sterling's laudable actions. This rescue was later highlighted in a newspaper column titled "Uncle Sam at Your Service." The piece in the *News-Press* of Fort Myers, Florida, featured illustrated panels that explained how Sterling rallied to the disaster and signaled the passing steamer. The article also praised "the gallant action of the lone keeper at the Craney Island Light."[178]

In October 1927, Sterling once again demonstrated his consummate professionalism when he came to the aid of women and children aboard a disabled launch near the station. Later that same year, as the *Defiance* transported cotton, apparently an errant cigarette landed on the baled fiber. In a flash, the boat became an inferno before individuals could reach the lifeboats. A memo to the commandant of the coast guard Rear Admiral Frederick C. Billard concluded, "Sterling greatly endangered his own life for

The busy port of Norfolk on the Elizabeth River, circa 1930. *Author's collection.*

he was compelled to row close to the burning boat…and there was a strong probability of the cargo of cotton exploding any instant. He was slightly burned by the blazing cotton."[179]

In the disaster, Sterling left the Craney Island Lighthouse in a small boat and headed for five men. One of the men panicked and jumped in the water, and Sterling rescued him. The boat burned the keeper as he approached, and he was at risk of being engulfed in a potential explosion. A passing motorboat secured the other men. The tender USLHT *Juniper* took the stranded crew to Norfolk. Meanwhile, the floating, blazing bales illuminated the scene.[180]

For this feat, the keeper earned another silver lifesaving medal of honor with a second service bar. Although, according to a memo sent to Billard, it appears Sterling's life was at risk and may have merited a gold lifesaving medal. In 1932, Sterling retired after more than thirty years of service, and the following year, the lighthouse was shuttered. In 1936, the district removed the structure and automated Craney Island by positioning a signal on the iron framework. In 1967, the brave keeper died at the age of ninety. The *Daily Press* noted on "seven different occasions Mr. Sterling was commended by the department and bureau and twice he was awarded life saving [*sic*] medals." He was buried in Forest Lawn Cemetery in the city of Norfolk, the same port where he often rallied to save its citizens and mariners.[181]

8

LAMBERT POINT

Quarantine and Coal, 1871

The creation of the Lambert Point Lighthouse in 1871 coincided with emergence of the maritime activity along the Elizabeth River. Congress budgeted $15,000 for the screwpile project. The light rested on a sandbar off Lambert Point (now Norfolk) in about three feet of water more than one thousand feet from the shipping channel. The depth of ten feet was not reached until one was about one hundred feet from the station. There were five piles driven for this station rather than the normal six. This resulted in the uneven settlement of the station, and stopgap measures were made to correct the problem. In 1874, according the *Alexandria Gazette*, the State of Virginia formally deeded land "on the shoal meking [*sic*] out into Elizabeth river from Lambert's Point."[182]

In 1873, it was reported that the foundation settled unevenly due to the missing sixth pile and soft river bottom. So, the lighthouse sat at a tilt; it was about fourteen inches lower on the west side. The remaining screwpiles were lowered, and four piles were added to balance the structure. During the stabilization process, crews added a dock from the shore and a pier. This station, along with the one on Craney Island, demarked quarantine anchorages for incoming vessels. A few years after the light first shone, the Norfolk Board of Health sought to fix a sign to it that consisted "of a board ten feet long, two feet wide painted yellow and bearing the word 'quarantine'…the board to be fixed on a spar driven into the bottom of the river."[183]

At Lambert Point, William D. Clegg (1876–83) and J.V. Clegg (1876–82) served as keepers. That decade's events that unfolded explained the

A U. S. BATTLESHIP IN DRY DOCK, NORFOLK NAVY YARD, NORFOLK, VA.

In the early 1900s, the warships built and maintained by the Norfolk Naval Yard steamed by Lambert Point into Hampton Roads and beyond. *Author's collection.*

value of the station. When the steamer *Isaac Bell* collided with the sloop *Katie Grant*, the impact tossed the sloop's captain into the freezing river. A passing vessel rescued the mariner and took him to the Lambert Point Lighthouse. The lighthouse staff tended to the skipper's chill and leg injury and also anchored the sloop near the lighthouse. The following year, in 1877, gripped by a squall, the sloop *California* capsized near the Craney Island Lighthouse. Once again, the steamer *Isaac Bell* sent a boat into the disaster and transported the crew to the point. The following day, William D. Clegg took the survivors to Norfolk. Clegg also became involved in the rescue efforts when the steamship *William Lawrence* collided with the packet-sloop *Three Sisters* from Chuckatuck. The sloop carried a deck full of sheep, but the flock was uninjured by the falling mast. A tug towed the damaged sloop, sheep and all, to the city as the head keeper transported the captain and crew.[184]

In the summer of 1880, the excitement came directly to Clegg at the station. A sloop collided with the station and upset the lamp. Keeper Clegg quickly returned the apparatus to its proper position, and the damage was minimal. A few days later, a crew member of the schooner *Sea Breeze* approached the lighthouse for matches. While returning to the schooner, the two boats collided, and the seaman was poured into the river while the schooner's tack moved the *Sea Breeze* away from the distressed man. Clegg lowered the station's boat and rescued the man.[185]

Amid this activity, coal piers mushroomed at the point. The Norfolk and Western Railroad Company's pier complex extended to the lighthouse and grew to be a rival of the Chesapeake and Ohio facility in Newport News. The Light House Board did not object to the endeavor, as long as the signal station maintained its integrity. Not surprisingly, the massive pier, with its own illumination, soon eclipsed the lighthouse. Objections were raised concerning the impact of the river's current by those not linked to the coal industry, but the growth continued. In April 1887, the *Baltimore Sun* reported the facility had recently loaded more than 650 various vessels with more than nine hundred thousand tons of coal.[186]

As the coal complex grew, the lighthouse's decline was accented by its off-kilter appearance. In 1887, the *Norfolk Landmark* called the signal "unsightly" and joined the list of institutions that recommended abandoning the lighthouse. By the close of 1892, the beacon at Lambert Point was useless. The new year started with no light functioning. The treasury's annual report from 1893 noted the removal of the lens, fog bell and all accoutrements to the Lazaretto Depot in Baltimore. The railroad company even attempted to

The massive Norfolk and Western coal piers eventually masked Lambert Point Lighthouse. Ironically, sailing vessels, like the schooner shown here, transported the coal to other destinations. *Author's collection.*

buy the lighthouse property. Starting in 1901, the station reemerged as a fog signal mounted on a steel skeleton tower with a one-half-horsepower motor driving the striker. The striker hit the half bell every five seconds.[187]

In 1924, the lighthouse district superintendents gathered in Norfolk for their annual meeting. Along with a tour of the innovations at Cape Henry, the supervisors visited Lambert Point. The point of interest was the fog signal's hygroscopic element. That is how the system determined the moisture saturation point in the atmosphere to initiate the signal. The Fifth District engineer developed the system using human hair—more specifically, what the *Lighthouse Service Bulletin* described as "part of a Chinaman's queue." When it was wet enough, it served as a contact to complete the circuit to start the automatic signal. As the hair dried, the circuit was broken, and the signal ceased to sound. The article offered no reason why the hair of an Asian male was sought or required.[188]

Already overshadowed and in decline, the tower with the fog signal collapsed during the Great Depression. The federal government held on to the site for two more decades. And then in 1957, the original five acres of property, described in the *Daily Press* as lying "600 yards off-shore and 35 feet under water [*sic*]," was returned to the state, still in the shadow of the coal piers.[189]

9

THIMBLE SHOAL

A Magnet for Drama, 1872

Mariners and superstitions have sailed together for centuries. Bad luck has been manifested by tales such as those of Davy Jones locker and the *Flying Dutchman*. To check these omnipresent evils, sailors flashed tattoos and carried cauls. Taking a different tack to safeguard vessels, federal authorities constructed lighthouses. Through this effort, towers of light became symbols of faith. And one of those hope-filled beacons signaled at Thimble Shoal as a guide to Hampton Roads in the Chesapeake Bay. This aid to navigation operated over the decades as a buoy, a lightship, a screwpile lighthouse and a caisson tower. Yet these lights that represented forward thinking were continually plagued with bad fortune in and around their stations. Horseshoe Bar off Fort Monroe included the "Thimble." Its sticky bottom was covered by about two fathoms of water. The *American Coast Pilot* of 1822 described it as "a small lump" that was quickly passed but remained a danger.[190]

At the outbreak of the Civil War, the Confederates removed this lightship from view of the federally held Fort Monroe. The federal Light House Board responded by anchoring a red nun (two cones) buoy, labeled "Thimble" on two sides with black letters. As the conflict progressed, the roadstead became a staging area for numerous amphibious operations down the south Atlantic coast, so marking this shoal was critical.[191]

In 1872, the Light House Board erected a screwpile lighthouse on the shoal. Like many of these arachnoid-like supports, the beacon took on the

In the early 1900s, the screwpile light at Thimble Shoal shown on this postcard was also known as "Bug Light." *Author's collection.*

additional name of "Bug Light." During the evening of October 30, 1880, the lighthouse caught fire. The *Richmond Dispatch* reported the structure "took fire this morning from a pipe running through the roof." Keeper "Captain" John Brown and Assistant Keeper Alexander G. Lee could not contain the blaze, so they departed in a boat for Fort Monroe.[192]

The district headquarters in Baltimore dispatched the USLHT *Tulip* to the scene. In Baltimore, work began immediately to reconstruct the razed screwpile station on the existing brown piles in about eleven feet of water. The plan was to assemble in Baltimore and then disassemble the house before transporting the structure. The final reassembly was expected to take about fourteen days. The rebuilt hexagonal white structure signaled white and red flashes. The lantern room was black, and the light was visible for almost twelve nautical miles. There were two fog bells, one on the north side and another on the south side.[193]

At the end of August 1886, the Charleston earthquake rumbled up through Hampton Roads and tested the new lighthouse. The quake was felt as far north as Boston. The unidentified keeper at Thimble Shoal felt a "slight" impact around 2:00 p.m. Interestingly, the keeper at nearby Old Point Comfort implied the quake hit about seven hours later. The Thimble Shoal keeper thought maybe a small craft or debris had collided with the piles of his station. Upon inspection, it appeared nothing struck the lighthouse "and that no damage had occurred."[194]

In the 1880s, Black lighthouse keepers began to man the station. These assistant keepers included John M. Chisman, Samuel Thornton, Southey Parker and Alexander G. Lee. Parker later served as the head keeper at Back River. Lee had formerly served at Old Point Comfort. Commander Robley D. Evans claimed Lee was unfit for duty and removed him from office. The local port collector also made specific allegations of drunkenness and sleeping while on duty. At this point, Senator William Mahone intervened on Lee's behalf and moved to punish Evans. Secretary of the Navy William Chandler, a Republican, cut Evans's pay for this issue. Despite the rebuke, Evans's career was not ruined.[195]

A railroad engineer and former Confederate general, Mahone, after the Civil War, was a leader in Virginia's Readjuster faction when he became a U.S. senator. The Readjusters attempted to unite white Republicans and recently enfranchised Black male voters. As an independent, Mahone held power in Congress, despite his junior status, because of the balanced party representation. By supporting the Republicans, Mahone was able to obtain key committee appointments for himself and hundreds of federal jobs in the commonwealth, which he shared with his political backers.[196]

Lee was not the only assistant to be cashiered in that era. In 1889, the district inspector reported J.W. Evans for "desertion and taking out of the post-office and carrying away with him the quarterly salary check of the Keeper." The draft had been cashed, and the inspector looked to recover the money. The request for "immediate removal of Evans" appears to have been honored.[197]

President Theodore Roosevelt appointed Rear Admiral Evans as the first commanding officer of the Great White Fleet, destined to circumnavigate the globe. The trek started after the Jamestown Exposition and involved navy ships that were painted white as a mark of distinction. The squadrons anchored across Hampton Roads and passed in review of Roosevelt and his party on board the presidential yacht *Mayflower* (PY 1), which was resting near the Thimble Shoal Lighthouse. Once the proceedings began, the *Daily Press* announced, the *Mayflower* led "the way to the reviewing water of Thimble Shoal Lighthouse." The overseas adventure lasted fourteen months, and many of the warships returned to Hampton Roads.[198]

Not long after the departure of the mighty fleet, a *Virginian-Pilot* journalist appeared to leap at the opportunity to describe a tempest-torn shipwreck. In late January 1908, the reporter told of the demise of the

Rear Admiral Robley D. Evans and President Theodore Roosevelt, in December 1907, gathered on the presidential yacht USS *Mayflower* (PY 1). *Library of Congress.*

A postcard of the naval personnel who became synonymous with Hampton Roads, circa 1900. *Author's collection.*

Uncle Sam, George Washington and Theodore Roosevelt welcome the return of the Great White Fleet, 1909. *Library of Congress.*

barge *Mascot*, noting the unfolding events were "reading like the page of a novel, or reminding one of a stage play." The opening scene had the tug *Bohemia* towing coal barges through extremely rough weather. Apparently, amid the turmoil an unidentified schooner cut the hawser, and the waves began to swap a stranded barge. As the barge began to sink, the captain was at the wheel and his brother on the watch. He directed his wife and child topside and into a yawl. The skipper then headed for the lighthouse.[199]

From the light, Keeper Walter Shawn and an assistant crewed their own small craft to move toward the yawl. The *Virginian-Pilot* commented at this action: "As brave as ever lived have charge of Uncle Sam's Beacon at the Thimbles." The keepers snatched the woman and child from the sinking boat and carried them to "refuge in the lighthouse." While discussing the rescue with a reporter, Captain Middleton struggled to describe the effort to save his family. Later, when Shaun's hometown newspaper the *Mathews Journal* reprinted the story, the editor added the banner "Capt. Shawn a Hero[,] Saves a Barge's Crew from a Watery Grave."[200]

AGROUND IN CHESAPEAKE BAY.

U. S. YACHT MAYFLOWER.

PRESIDENT'S YACHT MAYFLOWER ASHORE NEAR THIMBLE LIGHT

Navy Department Said To Have Ordered Investigation--Vessel Declared Not To Have Pilot Aboard.

Advices obtainable up to last midnight from Thimble light were to the effect that the President's yacht Mayflower, ashore there, had not been floated, but is expected that she will again be in deep water on high tide this morning.

A dispatch from Washington last night was that the Navy Department would order an investigation, fixing the responsibility for the grounding. The Mayflower was in command of Lieut.-Com. Carl T. Vogelgesang. The vessel, it is understood, went ashore during a fog.

The Mayflower, at the time she struck, was bound from the Washington navy yard to the navy yard here for repairs. She is to convey Mrs. Roosevelt, wife of the President, who will take in the Mardi Gras at New Orleans.

When the news of the mishap was sent here the naval tugs Pennacook, Hercules and Wahneta were sent down from the navy yard to assist the Mayflower. The colliers Nero and Brutus, which were in Hampton Roads, also went alongside of the yacht. It is stated that the position of the Mayflower is not dangerous. Late last night there was a thick haze prevailing, a light wind and not much of a sea.

GARABALDI GROUNDED IN SOUTHERN BRANCH

Evidence of Need of Deeper Channel and Work On Shoals.

That this port should have a greater depth of water, especially in the southern branch of the Elizabeth river, was demonstrated by the grounding of the Norwegian steamer Garabaldi, which vessel draws but fourteen feet of water, yet she hit on a shoal. Of course this would not have happened in the channel down the river, but it simply affords an illustration of some of the needs of the port.

The Garabaldi came in yesterday from Jacksonville to complete a cargo of lumber for Amherst, Nova Scotia, and went to the southern branch piers of the Virginian Railway. This lumber was left over from a recent call of the steamer, and it was on the previous trip that the Garabaldi hit bottom.

It is pointed out that on the southern branch of the Elizabeth river are located many enterprises which call for vessels, and that there should be a sufficient depth of water. One or two groundings, marine men say, will likely be the means of keeping vessels out, since no owner desires to take risks that involve their vessels.

Mayflower (PY 1) was grounded on Thimble Shoal while conveying the president's wife, Edith Kermit Carow Roosevelt, to New Orleans. *From the* Virginian-Pilot, *March 5, 1908.*

Later that same year, the *Mayflower*, with First Lady Edith K. Roosevelt, headed toward Hampton Roads. The evening weather was calm with a dense haze when the yacht ran aground. The story in the *Daily Capital Journal* blared, "The President's Yacht Is Aground," though crews on naval tugs and colliers determined the vessel was in no danger. The yacht was later towed to the Norfolk Navy Yard, and an inquiry followed. The press made a meal out of the mishap. The *Hawaiian Star* jeered, a "reporter asked the naval officials how it happened that so capable a Cmdr. ran aground. The reply was, 'Well, you didn't want him to hit the lighthouse did you? He merely went into the mud. No good navigator would hit a lighthouse.'"[201]

At the close of the same year, an employee at the district headquarters in Baltimore had a vivid dream. His slumbers provided him with a foreshadowing of the destruction of the Thimble Shoal Lighthouse. The next day, he passed along the details of the nightly vision to his coworkers. The *Baltimore American* claimed "he had dreamed that he came to the office to arrange for the plans for a new lighthouse at Thimble Shoals [*sic*]." His colleagues mocked him until a telegram arrived telling of the destruction of the lighthouse. Silence followed.[202]

The ethereal calamity that loomed in the draftsman's dreams manifested itself at the southern end of the bay. The tug *John Twohy, Jr.* towed the four-masted schooner *Malcolm Baxter, Jr.* toward Hampton Roads. With a shifting wind, the schooner veered toward the light. The captain of the tug realized the sailing vessel was on course to crush the wooden structure. Therefore, he released the connecting hawser with the expectation that the schooner would miss the beacon. Instead, the jibboom smashed through the upper lantern room and knocked one of the keepers off his feet while he was cleaning the lantern. A stove overturned, and the station was soon burning out of control. The two assistant keepers took to one of the station's boats. Meanwhile, the *Baxter* separated from the inferno without catching fire. The flames illuminated the winter skies and attracted a crowd along the shores of Fort Monroe. Close by vessels headed for the disaster and rescued the keepers. By the next morning, all that remained of the lighthouse were twisted iron piles.[203]

Red and white lights marked the wreckage as a navigational hazard. The first thought was to replace the beacon with a new lighthouse. This apparently, however, did not happen. Instead, a structure that was already built for another light was redirected to Hampton Roads. The white makeshift structure soon rested on top of the twisted metal. The new configuration downgraded the former fourth-order lens to a sixth-order lens, flashing red and white every ten seconds. The fog bell signal was struck every five seconds. The USLHT *Jessamine* acted as a tender during the early restructuring of the station. Then the following year, in 1911, another barge, the *Edward A. Schear*, struck the station while it was in tow by the *Prudence*. The tug and barge owners paid just over $1,000 for the damage.[204]

Given the fate of the two previous wooden lighthouses at Thimble Shoal, the Light House Board decided to build a caisson light adjacent to the old site. These sturdy structures look like sparkplugs or a teapot without a spout or handle. This light has several unusual features for a light in the bay area, most notably, diamond-shaped panes in its lantern and round portholes.

The massive construction project required an iron crib or pier filled with supporting concrete. A pneumatic process removed the fine white sand from the shoal and allowed the lighthouse to rest more than twelve feet below sea level. The truncated cone measured forty-two feet in diameter at the base and tapered slightly to thirty feet at the top. A tug took the cone from a marine railway in Berkley (Norfolk) to Thimble Shoal. The lighthouse had three floors. The top deck, which included a walking galley railing and veranda roof, expanded more than thirty-eight feet. Up to thirty feet from the base of the tower, 350 tons of riprap were to provide support and protection. A few years later, another 800 tons were added to the foundation.

While mariners touted Thimble Shoal as a critical station, the government was slow to replace the makeshift beacon with a proper lighthouse. The first monetary appropriation was not enough to complete the new caisson structure. At one point, construction stopped until Congress appropriated additional funds. As crews labored, the old screwpile framework served as the staging platform for the project. During construction, tragedy again embraced the station. A misunderstanding concerning the request for air instead sent water rushing into the cone. The six-man crew scrabbled upward, and two workers were injured. Foreman Ivanhoe Cabell of Norfolk struck his head on a bolt and slipped into the water. Rescuers managed to get the thirty-year-old foreman out of the tank, but he died shortly thereafter.[205]

Like they did for the screwpile lighthouse, three keepers maintained the light. The structure itself included two iron cisterns in the basement, rooms for engines, coal, oils and provisions and a water closet toilet. Two side hatch doors to the basement allowed for easier offloading of supplies from tenders. The entrance hall, kitchen, pantry, closets and living room were located on the first floor. There were two bedrooms and a storeroom on the second floor. The third floor held closets, another bedroom and the watch room. Connecting the tower was an enclosed four-story cylinder stair. There were ladders and two sets of davits for both vessels.

The lights featured six panels that revolved on ball bearings. The Fresnel lens and incandescent oil-vapor lamp combined to produce a forty-six-thousand-candlepower light. The focal plane was a tad over fifty-five feet high and could be seen from a distance of thirteen miles on a clear day.

Thimble Shoal Lighthouse near completion in 1914, with the screwpiles of the damaged light serving as a working platform and temporary beacon. *The Mariners' Museum.*

The fog signal was a third-class reed horn sounded by compressed air generated by kerosene engines. The signal was a one-second blast followed by four seconds of silence. There was also a mushroom trumpet signal. The construction took four years to complete a permanent tower at a cost of about $100,000. There were delays blamed on the weather, but in December 1914, the light was finished. The following year, the temporary light alongside the new tower was removed, but the supports of the screwpile were left. The skeletal remains were not removed until the beginning of the twenty-first century, and they have since become a favorite spot for anglers.[206]

While America remained neutral at the outbreak of World War I, the conflict quickly found its way to Hampton Roads. Under strict restrictions, German cruisers, such as the SMS *Prinz Eitle Friedrich*, sought the shelter and supplies that could be obtained in neutral ports, such as Newport News, Norfolk and Portsmouth. Meanwhile, British Royal Navy warships patrolled just off the coast, waiting for German ships to depart. Later, the merchant submarine *Deutschland* stopped in Hampton Roads on the way to Baltimore. The sub brought mail for the *Eitle*'s crew and medical supplies and dyes to America. The *Daily Press* announced, "*Deutschland* was reported off Thimble Shoals about four or five miles from Ft. Monroe." When the United States joined the Allies in 1917, the army laid torpedo nets between Forts Monroe and Wool and a second net line at Thimble Shoal. No ship was to anchor between the nets.[207]

Amid this tension, in the summer of 1918, Keeper Homer C. Groom and Assistant Keeper Benjamin D. Preston scrambled to a disabled motorboat with a half-dozen passengers about a half mile from the station. The motorboat was towed to Hampton. At this time, under Groom's leadership, the station earned the efficiency flag. Both men became career lighthouse keepers. Preston was among the long line of keepers from the southern tip of Mathews County.[208]

In 1921, the keepers were active in a variety of rescue efforts. The trio assisted the tug *Summit* when it lost a propeller wheel. That same year, two fishermen abandoned a sinking fishing steamer and then ran into trouble in a smaller boat. Keepers J.T. Twiford and Morgan saved the fishermen and the boat. A few years later, Meekins aided the *Sunbeam* and towed the yacht into Hampton. Meekins was also acknowledged for assisting a drifting motor launch without an anchor or fuel. Meekins and Morgan towed a disabled yacht to the safety of Willoughby Beach. In 1927, Twiford and Meekins even aided a naval pilot in a seaplane that landed near the lighthouse.[209]

The *Light List* from 1940 described the tower as resting in ten feet of water and able to send a white signal every two seconds that could be seen from distance of thirteen miles. Following the Japanese attack on Pearl Harbor, the United States joined the Allies and made Hampton Roads a nexus of martial activity. Naval bases, coal piers, army camps, railroads and shipyards operated twenty-four hours a day. All the while, the threat of German U-boats loomed off the Atlantic coast. The response to this threat manifested

Thimble Shoal Lighthouse, 1944. *The Mariners' Museum.*

as aerial reconnaissance, beach patrols, manning coastal and antiaircraft artillery and installing protective nets. Related activities also included live fire exercises and laying mines near the lighthouse. And while no enemy submarines attacked Hampton Roads, the federal government did secretly inter the remains of German submariners who lost their lives off the North Carolina coast in Hampton's national cemetery. The global war came to a close in 1945, when Japanese officials signed the instrument of surrender on USS *Missouri* (BB 63), also known as the "Mighty Mo," in Tokyo Bay.[210]

The "Mighty Mo" remained in active service after the war, and on a sunny morning in mid-January 1950, it steamed from Hampton Roads. The Thimble Shoal keepers may have then observed one of the most unnerving and awesome occurrences in the station's eventful history when *Missouri* veered from the main channel. The navigation officer took a quick bearing on the Thimble Shoal Lighthouse, but the massive vessel still imbedded itself in the shoal—at high tide no less. Communication failures among the ship's officers and misunderstandings that involved the new acoustical and traditional spar buoys contributed to the disaster.[211]

On January 17, 1951, battleship *Missouri* (BB 63) ran hard aground near Thimble Shoal Lighthouse for almost two weeks. The ship was freed with the assistance of twenty-three vessels. *National Archives and Records Administration.*

The press and other armed services had a field day. The battle wagon became known as the "Muddy Mo." Wags mocked: "Join the Navy and See Thimble Shoal!" An editorial cartoonist compared the warship to a stubborn "Show Me" state mule that refused to budge. Officers at Fort Monroe watched the unfolding drama from their beachfront club. Air force pilots from Langley Field got a bird's-eye view of the entire harbor. Civilians at Buckroe Beach flocked to the shore to experience the spectacle. As days passed, one entrepreneur considered ferrying tourists to the site. The circling coast guard cutters, however, would have curtailed their outings. Through it all, the caretakers at the Thimble Shoal Lighthouse had the best seat in the house. The tower even became a fifty-five-foot-tall "tripod" for photographing the mishap.[212]

To overcome the calamity, the U.S. Navy offloaded the crew, fuel, oil and munitions. The first few attempts to free the vessel failed. Rear Admiral Homer N. Wallin, a master salvager who cleared Pearl Harbor following the Japanese attack, developed the comprehensive plan, which employed divers and the application of pontoons, heavy rope wire, army dredges and tugs to free the nation's only commissioned battleship. Once freed, on February 1, the ship was guided by tugs to the Norfolk Navy Yard. Minor damage to the hull may have been caused by old wrecks in the shoal.[213]

With the *Missouri*'s departure, life at the station resumed a predictable routine. The keepers worked three weeks on, six days off. They stood hourly watches—eight on and eight off. A break in routine came with trips to the Fort Monroe commissary in the twenty-three-foot-long cabin boat

Henry T. Sharp Jr. took this shot of the schooner yacht *Sea Toy II* crossing the Thimble Shoal Lighthouse. In 1952, this image earned first place as a color transparency at The Mariners' Museum's fifth annual Exhibit of Marine Photography. *The Mariners' Museum.*

or sixteen-foot-long dinghy. Two generators provided electrical power for appliances and illumination. As years passed, more and more lighthouses became automated. A story in the *Virginian-Pilot* in the fall of 1961 described the activities, responsibilities and interests of the three coast guardsmen. Boatswain First Class Preston F. Meekins from Coinjock, North Carolina, managed the administrative affairs and enjoyed fishing, swimming, writing letters, playing cards, listening to the radio and watching television. Seaman W.E. Daisey was the cook, and dinner often included bluefish, trout, perch, seabass and rockfish. Coastguardsman Wright rounded out the team. "All agreed that lighthouse duty 'is not bad but a little lonely at times.'" At the time, the station had bells to back up the foghorn. An older Aladdin mantle was the substitute for the electric light, and it had a 250-watt bulb. The lamp system produced twenty-thousand-candlepower light. Three years later, the coast guard automated the station.[214]

The coast guard, of course, continued to maintain the tower and lamp, but without a permanent staff, the light station deteriorated. Meanwhile, seabirds roosted on the lighthouse, the paint peeled, its ladders and railings rusted and its floors buckled. In 1988, the officers and crew from USCGC *Red Cedar* (WLM 688) came to the rescue with a one-hundred-foot barge for support. On the floating platform, they installed a trailer and two toilets. They also hauled aboard a crane, sandblasters, generators and a dozen metal drums containing air hoses, paint, primer and lubricating oil. The crew remained on the job during the overhaul. At night, they secured the equipment, played spades and listened to the radio. As with most lights, the original Fresnel lens has been removed, replaced by more modern beacons; in this case, the lens is now displayed at the Coast Guard Training Center in Yorktown, Virginia. In 2005, under the National Historical Preservation Act of 2002, the lighthouse was sold at a government online auction to Peter Jurewicz of Suffolk, Virginia, for a winning bid of $65,000.[215]

10

NANSEMOND RIVER

Suffolk Sentry, 1878

During the Civil War, Surgeon James A. Mowris of the 114th New York described the Nansemond River as "exceedingly devious. It doubles upon itself so repeatedly, that I do not doubt but there are sections of it which will represent every letter of the alphabet. [The] river *is* very crooked, marshy on both sides and full of oysters." When peace came, there was a rise in water traffic to Suffolk, as the lumber trade and demand for local seafood rose. Much of that movement involved planting, harvesting and transporting oysters. Communities such as Eclipse and Crittenden thrived on the shellfish trade. As early as 1866, the schooners *Leading Breeze*, *J.C. Curtis* and *Eunice P. Newcomb* transported Nansemond River oysters to northern ports like Boston and New Haven. Not only were there vast numbers of the bivalve, but a government report (1869) claimed the "oysters of Tangiers are excelled in delicious flavor by those at the mouth of the James and the Nansemond Rivers."[216]

In this environment in 1878, the federal government decided to locate the Nansemond River Lighthouse about a half-mile north of Pig Point at the mouth of the river in about six feet of water. The hexagonal screwpile structure was framed at the district's Lazaretto Depot in Baltimore and then packed and loaded on board the USLHT *Tulip*. Part of the new light's framework came from the station at Roanoke Marshes in North Carolina. Engineers determined the bottom of the river was too hard to use screwpiles, so the supports of wooden piles encased in iron-cast sleeves were affixed using pneumatic pressure. Despite this variant, the structure

Nansemond River Lighthouse. *The Mariners' Museum.*

was still described as a screwpile lighthouse. The sixth-order red light was originally fueled by mineral oil and flashed for thirty-six feet about the river. In 1899, a new fifth-order Fresnel lens was installed to replace the smaller sixth-order lens.[217]

From 1878 to 1892, at least four Black keepers served at the station. Most of these men were politically active around their respective tenures at the

Nansemond River Lighthouse. Starting in 1881, Principal Keeper William A. Bond earned $540 per year and started as an assistant at the same station. Assistant Keeper Exum White remained involved in Republican politics for more than twenty years. In 1902, he worked with John S. Wise to challenge the new state constitution that disfranchised so many Black voters.[218]

Starting at the end of the nineteenth century, keepers from Mathews began to populate the station. At least ten Mathews men tended the light. One of these reliable men was J. Filmore Hudgins. While in the grip of the winter of 1896, Hudgins received a stunning message. His family physician telegrammed: "Your Child Gertrude burnt yesterday. No chance of recovery." The Light House Service allowed leave for such emergencies if there was at least one keeper at the station. Substitute keepers could maintain the light in a pinch. Hudgins was able to return to his family during the crisis, and the doctor's prognoses was incorrect. Gertrude Hudgins survived the accident, and Assistant Keeper Hudgins returned to the light. Keeper Temple Ripley, another Mathews keeper, was awarded the lighthouse efficiency pennant. He resigned from the station around 1926 due to health issues.[219]

The turn of the century also brought a new signature to the lighthouse. In 1899, the lens was upgraded to a stronger light fixture. The *Light List* of 1907 described the lens as being thirty-six feet tall with a sixth-order lens with a fixed red signal. In 1935, the last year of service for the

Principal Keeper J. Filmore Hudgins and his daughter Gertrude. *Courtesy of Cindy Hudgins Brizzolara.*

280-candlepower light, the signal was forty feet above the water, signaling for ten seconds (a flash lasting one second followed by a nine-second eclipse). The coast guard removed the old light and replaced the structure with a new support and signal.[220]

Like other lights along the James River, the Nansemond River Lighthouse went through numerous reconfigurations around the time of World War II. In the summer of 1941, the light changed to a flashing white light every five seconds and then a one-second flash followed by a four-second eclipse. Certainly because of weather concerns, starting in early January 1942, the light was extinguished, and keepers were allowed to leave their duties. The light appears to have been extinguished again after the war. The coast guard removed the structure and, until 1974, maintained a signal on its framework. The station was still a day mark and boundary. In 1979, a newspaper noted the oyster planting grounds near Pig Point were "Near [the] Nansemond River Lighthouse Frame."[221]

11

NEWPORT NEWS
MIDDLE GROUND

City Clarion, 1891

The Battle of Hampton Roads on March 8 and 9, 1862, gives historical perspective to the need for navigational aids and harbor pilots. During the Civil War, Union troops had extended westward from Fort Monroe on the Virginia Peninsula, and the U.S. Navy blockaded the roadstead. To the south, Confederate fortifications protected Norfolk and Portsmouth. On the first day of the battle, the ironclad CSS *Virginia* created mayhem. During the engagement, at least four warships ran aground: USS *Roanoke*, USS *Minnesota*, USS *St. Lawrence* and USS *Congress*. Wounded on the first day of the clash, Confederate flag officer Franklin Buchanan reported, "The Minnesota grounded in the north channel, where, unfortunately, the shoalness of the channel prevented our near approach."[222]

That evening, the ironclad the USS *Monitor*, Lieutenant John L. Worden commanding, arrived from Brooklyn. The preceding year, Worden had passed through Hampton Roads under different circumstances. Confederates captured the lieutenant after he delivered secret dispatches to federal commands in Florida. He was then exchanged at Hampton Roads. Surviving that ordeal, Worden returned to Virginia. Now as the captain of the Union ironclad, Worden faced, in his own words, "the very serious danger of grounding in the narrower portions of the channel and near some of the enemies." Despite the lack of a local pilot, the following day, the *Monitor* engaged its counterpart, the *Virginia*, for about four hours. During the duel, the *Virginia* grounded but was able to free itself. At the close of the engagement, a rebel shell shattered the *Monitor*'s viewing portal and temporarily blinded Worden.[223]

When the war ended, trade returned to the commonwealth. In 1871, the need for navigational aids on the curved, sandy shoal that had once trapped the likes of the *Minnesota* resurfaced. The first effort placed two horizontal-striped buoys on the ends of the narrow, mile-long channel. Authorities determined the emergence of larger vessels required more protection, especially when ship masters were reluctant to disembark at night or during adverse conditions. This delay cost shippers money. Meanwhile, railroad tycoon Collis P. Huntington acquired the land and the access points for his emerging Chesapeake and Ohio Railway on the peninsula to export Appalachian coal. In 1887, Newport News incorporated as a city. Huntington also established a boat repair yard (present-day Newport News Shipbuilding). The facility built its first tug in 1881, and in less than a decade, it launched, simultaneously, two warships. This activity fueled the need for more navigational improvements.[224]

Senator Mahone, the railway and the Virginia Pilot Association lobbied steadily for a Newport News light station. Boring samples found white sand underneath silt and mud. By 1888, both houses of Congress passed bills to construct the project, but the cost estimates varied. Once plans were approved, the request for proposals was made for the construction of a massive metal cylinder for the base of a lighthouse and its subsequent installation on the bar in fifteen feet of water. The original contract for the entire job allowed for a bid of about $50,000. However, on further review, the Light House Board's engineers concluded that a bid at this price for the original specifications left "too small a margin for the purchase of the materials to be supplied to the contractors by the government and for incidental and contingent expenses." Therefore, modifications in the substructure and the amount of riprap were reduced. These adjustments cut costs by $4,000.[225]

Described shortly after construction, the brown (later listed as brick-red) tower rested on a "black cylindrical foundation pier." Crews sunk the massive cylinder, measuring twenty-five feet in diameter and fifty-six feet in length, on a carefully selected location into a white oak and Virginia yellow pine caisson. The Newport News Middle Ground Lighthouse was the first caisson-based station built in Virginia and was of the same design as the Crabtree Ledge Lighthouse in Frenchman Bay, Maine. The style is commonly thought to resemble a coffeepot or sparkplug.[226]

The station had five levels (three habitable) with seven windows and included a cellar, sleeping quarters, storage lockers, an observation deck and

Newport News Middle Ground Lighthouse shortly after construction. *Gonsoulin and Billingsley families.*

watch and lantern rooms. There were also coal bunkers and two cisterns used to collect 2,700 gallons of rainfall. Its other features included a brick-lined interior, boats launched from davits and an exterior water closet.[227]

On April 15, 1891, the light became operational. Captain Dan Clayton of Newport News was appointed as an assistant keeper. The first head keeper was James Beauregard Hurst. When completed, the station featured a fourth-order lens that flashed a white light every twelve and a half seconds from a focal plane of fifty-two and a half feet, and a fog bell was struck with a double blow every fifteen seconds. The beacon flashed as a navigational sentinel alongside a bustling shipping channel. By 1907, the white light flashed every twenty seconds.[228]

All told, there were scores of principal or assistant keepers who tended to the station for sixty-three years. At least three of these men served as both assistant and head keepers. Hurst, Virgil J. Montague, Wesley F. Ripley, J. Filmore Hudgins, John F. Jarvis, Rufus Thomas Hunley and Charles F. Hudgins were among the Middle Ground keepers who hailed from Mathews County. The keepers or assistant keepers from the Outer Banks included

Henry H. Twiford, Theodore S. Twiford, Edward B. Austin, Charles B. Quidley, Martin B. Tolson, James B. Cox, Cleon C. Tillett and Arthur M. Meekins. Head Keeper Meekins summarized this Outer Banks legacy while completing a questionnaire: "I have been a boatman all my life before entering this service."[229]

One of the notable keepers was Old Dominion native James E. Llewellyn. He served as one of the early head keepers (1898–1904). He had previously worked at the York Spit Lighthouse before relocating his growing family to Newport News. After a six-year stint at Middle Ground, Llewellyn then took on the duties at nearby Back River before returning to Newport News as an assistant keeper. Llewellyn and his wife, Cora, established their home on Thirty-First Street, a few miles from the lighthouse—as the crow flies. Although, once on duty, Keeper Llewellyn was in a different world. In 1900, the keeper left behind a house full of people, including a daughter-in-law and a middle-aged roomer. Together, the couple had at least a dozen children, and twice, Cora gave birth to two children in the same year. Undoubtedly, Cora's duties as a housekeeper were as challenging as any lighthouse keeper's jobs.[230]

In 1901, James Llewellyn and his son Irving tended the station. Oddly, the teenager was listed as a "laborer" in the federal employee register, not

The expansion of the Newport News Shipbuilding and Drydock Company depended on navigation aids, such as the Newport News Middle Ground Lighthouse. *Author's collection.*

as an assistant keeper. Although, the youngster did earn an annual salary of $440, which was consistent with an assistant's pay for that era. Head keepers earned about $600 annually for the same period. The younger Llewellyn did not follow in his father's footsteps into the lighthouse service. Instead, he became a pastor. The senior Llewellyn followed his own calling as a lighthouse keeper for thirty years.[231]

The duties of the father-son team included maintaining the clockwork machinery, lamp, lens, fog signal, boats and chipping rust and painting. In addition, the keepers' duties included varnishing and scrubbing the heart pine floors. Their shifts lasted six hours, and normally, there were two men on duty at the station. On average, the light was illuminated for twelve hours a day. Weekly trips by a crew member ashore in the motor launch gathered mail and provisions. This chore normally took five to six hours. Lighthouse tenders in the district, such as the USLHT *Jessamine*, the USLHT *Violet* and the USLHT *Maple*, delivered food, oil, supplies and tons of coal. Tender crews also made repairs and dropped protective riprap to the base of the tower.

The same year Middle Ground Lighthouse first flashed in the harbor, there were almost five hundred schooner and close to nine hundred steamship landings made at Newport News. In addition, thirty-four barks and four sailing ships departed from the port. The schooners were part of the coastal and Caribbean trade and moved mostly coal but also transported lumber and grain. Smaller craft, such as log canoes, skipjacks, bugeyes, buy boats and Hampton flatties, added a local flavor as watermen harvested crabs and oysters.[232]

Business interests continued to lobby for local navigational upgrades. Federal engineers mapped a thirty-foot-deep channel through the bar and added gas markers. By 1900, these enhancements allowed the largest vessels to depart fully loaded at any time, no matter the tide. Nonetheless, the harbor could be dangerous. In 1909, SS *Alaska* ran aground just outside of the channel while transporting nine thousand tons of coal bound for San Francisco. This occurred despite the captain taking the precaution to sound the channel to make sure there was thirty feet of water. Still, during the actual voyage, the *Daily Press* claimed, the steamship "took an unexpected sheer when nearing the lighthouse and went a ship's length out of the channel and stuck fast on the bar." In 1912, hydraulic dredging operations deepened the channel to thirty-five feet. By the time of America's involvement in World War I, the enhancements made the channel six hundred feet wide and more than three miles long through the northern shoal near the Middle Ground Lighthouse.[233]

The casino and countless schooners were part of the growing activity in Newport News in the early twentieth century. *Author's collection.*

The waterfront of Newport News shortly after the construction of the Newport News Middle Ground Lighthouse. *Author's collection.*

This postcard marked the location of the Battle of Hampton Roads as a ferry crosses in front of the Newport News Middle Ground Lighthouse, circa 1920. *The Mariners' Museum.*

Crews also made improvements to the light station in 1898, when men of the *Jessamine* assisted in testing the audibility of the fog signal. Later, the tug *Minerva*, acting as a tender, deposited additional riprap around the tower. In 1912, the malfunctioning fog bell required it to be struck by hand in thick weather for ten days. That same year, the Middle Ground keepers earned an efficiency star. Three years later, Keeper Edward Farrow's diligent efforts earned the station a "star of silver." Farrow, a native of North Carolina, worked for more than fifteen years at Middle Ground, and in 1908, he became the head keeper. He and his wife, Minnie, resided for most of that time on Twenty-Third Street in Newport News.[234]

In early 1918, a cold snap seized the eastern United States amid World War I. The *Lighthouse Service Bulletin* lamented that "great damage has resulted to many lighthouse structures from ice conditions in the first to sixth districts, inclusive." Hampton Roads froze over. Ice drove ships off course, which forced them to drag their anchors ashore and onto bars. If Newport News Middle Ground Lighthouse was a screwpile station, the ice floes would have likely twisted the iron framework like rubber tubing and crushed the house into flotsam. The station's logbook gives some insight into the seasonal ordeal. In February, the keepers recorded: "Ice drifting all about...cold [,] freezing....Ice...heavy....Shaking Station Bad. PM Ice breaking up." Keepers "painted Red lead around bottom of Station wich [*sic*] ice had scaped [*sic*] off."[235]

Along with natural disasters, keepers were involved in a number of rescues. Assistant Keeper Carl G. Marsh rendered assistance to five passengers in a motorboat near the light. In a letter of commendation to Marsh, Acting Secretary of Commerce Edwin F. Sweet noted, "The department commends you for your service thus rendered." According to the *Lighthouse Service Bulletin*, in 1918, Head Keeper Malachi D. Swain towed a disabled boat to the light and assisted with engine repairs. The Jazz Age fueled a passionate interest in airplanes and runabouts. Speed and good judgment, however, often do not travel in tandem. In the winter of 1920, Head Keeper Swain and Assistant Keeper Martin B. Tolson rescued three travelers in a disabled motorboat after they had gotten lost in the fog, and he assisted in getting the craft to shore. In 1921, a motorboat collided with the lighthouse station's ladder during a storm, and Principal Keeper Homer Austin offered aid.[236]

Other tragedies and mishaps occurred during the Great Depression. Acting Assistant Keeper W.S. Brown, while working the Christmas season, rowed to the station with gifts, mail and good cheer for Assistant Keeper John B. Cox. Despite the rolling sea, the rower arrived safely, only to find Cox dead. Brown cooperated with the coroner, who determined the sixty-nine-year-old keeper had died of a heart attack on the afternoon of December 19, 1937. The experienced keeper left behind a wife and children. A death at a lighthouse meant the surviving keeper had to secure the remains in a structure surrounded by water. According to Welsh lighthouse lore, in the early 1800s, a keeper on Smalls Rock had to preserve remains for two weeks. A dangling arm of the deceased knocking on a window pane drove the living keeper mad. The following year, a pair of ordinary events at the Middle Ground Lighthouse blended to give the impression that the station was ablaze. A gleaming, fresh coat of paint and a brush fire directly behind the tower gave observers the impression that the structure was burning. But upon closer inspection, the would-be rescuers unraveled the illusion.[237]

With America's involvement in World War II, Hampton Roads became an extremely active port. The authorities established navigation restrictions for commercial vessels traveling around Middle Ground Lighthouse and on the Elizabeth River. Boatswain Mate First Class Edward B. Austin served as the head keeper and earned $1,560 annually. The Old North State native was in his late forties at the time, had an eighth-grade education and resided in Norfolk with his wife and children. The assistant keeper and coast guardsman

Left: This overhead view of Newport News Middle Ground Lighthouse demonstrates how the structure was also an aid to aerial navigation. *The Mariners' Museum.*

Below: Newport News Middle Ground Lighthouse, 1945. *The Mariners' Museum.*

William Gibbs, another North Carolinian, had already served at Middle Ground in the late 1920s before returning to tend the light for most of the war. He earned $1,440 annually, had completed one year of high school and resided with his family in Warwick County (present-day Newport News).[238]

Near the lighthouse, the shipyards boomed and military installations hummed. Operations such as the Horace E. Dodge Boat Works (also known as the Boat and Plane Corporation), which had closed during the Great Depression, reopened to manufacture landing craft. In October 1942, Major General George S. Patton's units departed Hampton Roads for North Africa. All told, more than thirty thousand soldiers embarked on transports at Newport News and were accompanied by escort ships across the Atlantic. Following early setbacks, the U.S. Army went on the offensive, captured members of the German Afrika Korps and sent those prisoners to Hampton Roads to be expressed to camps throughout the South.[239]

Following the war, social changes rippled through the nation's institutions. Among those changes was racial integration in the military services. With that in mind, Boatswain's Mate Third Class Cleon Curtis "Sunny" Tillett, in 1949, assumed his duties at the station. Prior to lighthouse duty, he served at the Pea Island Life-Saving Station in Rodanthe, North Carolina. For most of the facility's history, Black men, such as Tillett, manned the Pea Island facility. When the station closed, he became a "keeper" at Newport News Middle Ground. In August 1952, he signed his name "C.C. Tillett" as the "Officer in Charge" on a "miscellaneous events of the day" record concerning the hospitalization of another team member. With his assignment, Black men once again operated the region's light stations.[240]

The lighthouse continued to serve as a radio calibration station, sending out a signal at a frequency of three hundred kilocycles that could be heard from a ten-mile distance. Keeper Harvey E. Mayor, a native of Maryland, applied his skills as former radio operator to maintain this feature. Mayor had already served at four lighthouses and hoped to close his career at another light station, even though the number of manned stations was on the decline. Mayor had also served as a quartermaster on district lighthouse tenders, such as the USCG *Mistletoe*, and as an assistant keeper at the Old Plantation Flats station just before taking over at Middle Ground. Despite the multiple roles of the station, the coast guard elected to automate it. Keeper Mayor, Second Class Engineman William Walker and Seaman James Rhodes were the last to tend the light. The preparations that were made for closing Middle Ground included offloading a refrigerator and stove, furniture, gas cylinders, beds, lifesaving gear and fishing tackle.[241]

The last crew shared with a newspaper reporter their respective views on life at the Middle Ground Lighthouse. Mayor remarked how the sturdy station easily weathered Hurricane Hazel, how it was a great fishing spot and how quickly time flew there. Walker passed his off hours painting seascapes and patrol boats. Unfortunately, the departure of these "wickies" marked a decline in the care of the station. The coast guard soon reclassified the structure as a tall, second-class buoy. At the time of the station's automation, the timing of the light and bell signal were changed. The light, now on top of the tower on a pole, flashed white every six seconds. The buoy required a nine-day visitation cycle to attend to its batteries; otherwise, the station stood alone and became a victim of human recklessness and wildlife.[242]

Despite the efforts of the coast guard, the station degraded for the remainder of the twentieth century. In the spring of 1979, the tugboat *Capt. Jim*, while towing a barge, collided with the tower. In the 1980s, details sent to repair leaks, water damage and broken windows and to remove guano revealed how badly the structure was suffering from the lack of regular maintenance and positive human contact. It was also during this era that the coast guard added solar panels and moved the new light outside the lantern room. When the Monitor and Merrimac Memorial Bridge-Tunnel, another vehicular route across Hampton Roads, opened, its ribbon of white lights obscured the tower's illumination. To counter this problem, the coast guard moved the light inside the tower and, on July 7, 2000, changed the signal color to red.[243]

None of these adjustments to the light signal added to the protection of the Middle Ground Lighthouse despite its inclusion in the National Register of Historic Places. With that in mind, the National Historic Lighthouse Preservation Act (NHLPA) of 2000 allowed the government to pass along the ownership of light stations to other government agencies and private nonprofit organizations. The towers could then theoretically serve cultural functions while serving as navigational aids. For stations such as those at Thimble Shoal and Newport News Middle Ground, however, this was problematic. These structures rested in busy waterways, were designed to house only three people, needed extensive repairs and were only accessible by watercraft. Consequently, when agencies did not successfully secure the rights to the lights, individuals were allowed to bid on the stations.[244]

Fortunately for the station, in 2005, Bob and Joan Gonsoulin and Jackie and Daniel Billingsley purchased the Newport News's Middle Ground Lighthouse. Joan and Jackie are sisters, so the venture was a family undertaking. This was the first station to pass to private ownership under the NHLPA. Caveats for

Newport News Middle Ground Lighthouse, 1971. *Photograph by Marcus F. Ritger Jr.; the Mariners' Museum.*

Opposite, top: In the early 2000s, the restoration was in full swing as this painter operated from a bosun's chair. *Gonsoulin and Billingsley families.*

Opposite, bottom: Family and friends lean into nettle guns and air hammers to remove old paint and rust. *Gonsoulin and Billingsley families.*

Above: The Newport News Middle Ground Lighthouse shortly before restoration. *Gonsoulin and Billingsley families.*

the acquisition required coast guard access to the tower and compliance with guidelines from the state's Department of Historic Resources. The winning bid was $31,000, but the structure required extensive repairs and upgrades before it was habitable. An additional investment of more than $200,000 and seven thousand hours of labor was required. The expenses for restoration would have run considerably higher, but the extended families boasted engineers, a circle of go-getters, interested friends and hardworking engineering students.[245]

The four-year undertaking included cleaning up bird droppings, upgrading two cisterns, chipping lead-based paint and repainting and repairing portholes. There was plenty of heavy lifting, wooden floor refinishing and grinding metal before passing safety inspections. Improvements to the facility included: an interior marine toilet, a generator run by a bank of wet-cell batteries, a modern kitchen, an outdoor shower and new railings and ladders. Custom-made curved furniture, known as "banana bunks" in English lighthouses, accented the decor.

The bedroom of the restored Newport News Middle Ground Lighthouse. *Gonsoulin and Billingsley families.*

The Newport News Middle Ground Lighthouse after restoration. Note the solar panels for the light that are still maintained by the coast guard. *Gonsoulin and Billingsley families.*

Above: After four years of hard work, the Gonsoulin and Billingsley families and their friends enjoyed this unique waterfront destination. *Gonsoulin and Billingsley families.*

Left: A proud Joan Gonsoulin and the Newport News Lighthouse. The friends and families of sisters Joan Gonsoulin and Jackie Billingsley united to restore the structure. *Gonsoulin and Billingsley families.*

Members of the U.S. Coast Guard Aids to Navigation Hampton Roads relax after participating in a reenlisting ceremony at the Newport News Middle Ground Lighthouse. *Gonsoulin and Billingsley families.*

Finally, the mermaid and James River murals acknowledge the structure's salty setting, as is the timeline of the station's light keepers.[246]

The Billingsley-Gonsoulin team effort did not go unnoticed. Their collective undertaking was featured extensively in the local press, recreational living magazines and the Better Homes and Gardens network. The capstone of the project occurred on Fourth of July 2006, when "humanity overwhelmed the station in the best of ways." Since the lighthouse's opening, more than 1,700 guests have visited the station. And in a collective report to the author, the owners concluded, "Middle Ground Light has fulfilled the goals of the NLHPA, enabling private owners to transform a dirty and deteriorating structure into a charming residence that still serves as an aid to navigation."[247]

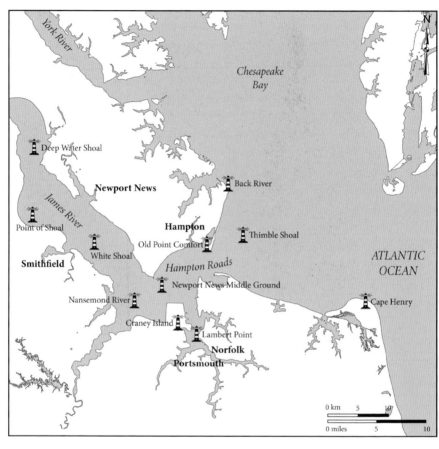

Above: Lighthouses of Southeastern Virginia. *George Chakvetadze, Alliance USA.*

Opposite: Lighthouses and landmarks of Hampton Roads. *George Chakvetadze, Alliance USA.*

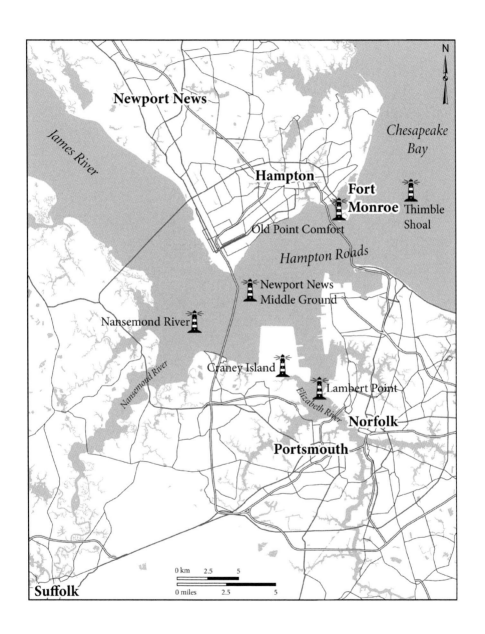

N

Newport News

James River

Chesapeake Bay

Hampton

Fort Monroe

Thimble Shoal

Old Point Comfort

Hampton Roads

Newport News Middle Ground

Nansemond River

Nansemond River

Craney Island

Lambert Point

Elizabeth River

Norfolk

Portsmouth

0 km   2.5   5

0 miles   2.5   5

Suffolk

NOTES

Chapter 1

1. Arthur Pierce Middleton, "The Struggle for the Cape Henry Lighthouse," *American Neptune* 8, no. 1 (January 1948): 26–28.
2. Kevin C. Valliant, "'Preservation…From the Dangers of the Enemy as Well as Seas': The Establishment of the Old Cape Henry Lighthouse," unpublished thesis, Old Dominion University, 1995, 22–29, 45–53, 72, 85; William H. Hening, *The Statutes at Large; Being a Collection of all the Laws of Virginia* (New York: R&W&G Barton, 1819), 6, 8, 227–29, 539–40; *Daily Press* (Newport News, VA), June 16, 1968.
3. Eric Jay Dolin, *Brilliant Beacons: A History of the American Lighthouse* (New York: Liveright, 2016), 55, 62–64; Dennis L. Noble, *Lighthouses & Keepers: The U.S. Lighthouse Service and Its Legacy* (Annapolis, MD: Naval Institute Press, 1997), 6; Valliant, "Preservation," 69–72.
4. Harold C. Syrett, ed., *The Papers of Alexander Hamilton*, vol. 6 (New York: Columbia University Press, 1962), 554; "Cape Henry Lighthouse, the First Lighthouse Build by the Federal Government," *Lighthouse Service Bulletin* 5, no. 37 (January 1939): 150; William P. Palmer and Sherwin McRae, eds., *Calendar of Virginia State Papers, July 2, 1790 to August 10, 1792*, vol. 4 (Richmond, VA: R.F. Walker, 1885), 265; Henry F. Withey and Elsie R. Withey, *Biographical Dictionary of Americans Architects* (Los Angeles, CA: New Age, 1956), 403–4; Valliant, "Preservation," 80–81; *Baltimore Sun*, August 1, 2003.

5. Theresa Levitt, *A Short, Bright Flash: Augustin Fresnel and the Birth of the Modern Lighthouse* (New York: W.W. Norton, 2013), 52; Tom Nancollas, *Seashaken Houses: A Lighthouse History from Eddystone to Fastnet* (London: Penguin, 2018), 111, 121; Candace Clifford, *Inventory of Historic Light Stations* (Washington, D.C.: National Park Service, 1994), 316; Valliant, "Preservation," 86–87.

6. George R. Putnam, "Beacons of the Sea," *National Geographic* 24, no. 1 (January 1913), 9 (quotation), 15 (There is a facsimile of Jefferson's letter [December 31, 1806] in this article); *Daily Press* (Newport News, VA), April 6, 1963; "First Lighthouse Build," *Lighthouse Service Bulletin*, 150; Valliant, "Preservation," 87–88.

7. B. Henry Latrobe, "Memoir on the Sand Hills of Cape Henry in Virginia," *William and Mary Quarterly* 14, no. 4 (April 1906): 257, 258 (quotation); Edward C. Carter II, et al., eds., *Latrobe's View of America, 1795–1820: Selections from the Watercolors and Sketches* (Baltimore: Maryland Historical Society, 1985), 150–55.

8. William S. Dudley, ed., *The Naval War of 1812: A Documentary History, 1813*, vol. 2 (Washington, D.C.: Naval Historical Center, 1992), 318, 345 (quotation), 352–54; *Evening Post*, July 20, 1813; Dolin, *Brilliant Beacons*, 76–77.

9. Robert H. Burgess, *Chesapeake Circle* (Cambridge, MD: Tidewater, 1965), 112; Robert Burts, *Around the World: A Narrative of a Voyage in East India Squadron*, vol. 1 (New York: Charles S. Francis, 1840), 20; Walter Colton, *Ship and Shore: Leaves from the Journal of a Cruise to the Levant* (New York: A.S. Barnes, 1835), 13.

10. Charles Thompson, "Bowe, or Three Months at a Cannibal Court," *Southampton Magazine* 1, no. 4 (Winter 1912): 5; *Sailor's Magazine and Naval Journal* 12 (February 1840): 195; *Sailor's Magazine and Naval Journal* 13 (June 1841): 325; Edmund M. Blunt, *American Coast Pilot*, 2nd ed. (Newburyport, MA: Edmund M. Blunt, 1798), 104–5 (Hereinafter *ACP*, published by Edmund M. Blunt, George Blunt and others in New York and other cities.); *ACP* (1822), 219.

11. *Journal and Papers of the Virginia State Convention of 1861*, vol. 3 (Richmond, VA: Virginia State Library, 1966), 48; *Baltimore Sun*, May 25, 1861; *Liverpool Mercury*, June 4, 1861; *New York Daily Herald*, January 27, 1862.

12. William H. Egle, *History of the Counties of Dauphin and Lebanon on the Commonwealth of Pennsylvania* (Philadelphia, PA: Everts and Peck, 1883), 106; A.T. Andreas, *History of the State of Kansas*, vol. 2 (Chicago: A.T. Andreas, 1883), 792; *Baltimore Sun*, July 11, 1863.

13. *Courier-Journal* (Louisville, KY), April 28, 1866; *Daily Standard* (Raleigh, NC), October 27, 1866; *Daily Press* (Newport News, VA), April 6, 1963; Clifford, *Historic Light Stations*, 316; *Report of the Secretary of the Treasury of the State on the Finances for the Year 1869* (Washington, D.C.: Government Printing Office, 1869), 447 (Hereinafter, *AR-Treasury*.).

14. Willis Augustus Hodges, *Free Man of Color: The Autobiography of Willis Augustus Hodges*, edited by Willard B. Gatewood Jr. (Knoxville: University of Tennessee Press, 1982), lxiv–lxvi; *Liberator* (Boston, MA), July 30, 1847; *Brooklyn Daily Eagle*, August 11, 1864.

15. *Norfolk Virginian*, October 11, 1867; *Norfolk Virginian*, November 11, 1871; *Norfolk Virginian*, September 4, 1878; *Richmond Dispatch*, October 28, 1867; Hodges, *Free Man of Color*, lxvii.

16. Cynthia M. Leonard, *The General Assembly of Virginia, July 30, 1619–January 11, 1978* (Richmond: Library of Virginia, 1978), 518, 522, 525, 530, 534, 539; *Norfolk Landmark*, November 25, 1880.

17. Steven Hahn, *A Nation Under Our Feet: Black Political Struggles in the Rural South from Slavery to the Great Migration* (Cambridge, MA: Belknap Press, 2003), 376–84; John F. Chappo, "William Mahone of Virginia: An Intellectual Biography, 1830–1890," unpublished dissertation, University of Southern Mississippi, 2007, 192, 198, 203; Sandra MacLean Clunies, "African American Lighthouse Keepers of the Chesapeake Bay," *AAHGS News* (September–October 2012), 9, 11–13; *Norfolk Virginian*, September 29, 1881. See also: *Weekly Virginian and Carolinian* (Norfolk, VA), August 9, 1883.

18. Thomas Parramore, et al., *Norfolk: The First Four Centuries* (Charlottesville: University Press of Virginia, 1994), 253; James T. Moore, "Black Militancy in Readjuster Virginia, 1879–1883," *Journal of Southern History* 41, no. 2 (May 1975): 170, 176–77; William H. Stewart, *A Pair of Blankets: War-time History in Letters*, edited by Benjamin H. Trask (1911; repr., Wilmington, NC: Broadfoot, 1990), 250–51; *Richmond Dispatch*, November 6, 1879; *Baltimore Sun*, March 3, 1881; *Norfolk Landmark*, September 14, 1881; *Norfolk Landmark*, November 25, 1880; *Norfolk Landmark*, December 14, 1881; *Daily Press* (Newport News, VA), January 31, 2021.

19. *Daily Press* (Newport News, VA), November 20, 1909.

20. *Daily Press* (Newport News, VA), April 12, 1929; *Daily Press* (Newport News, VA), April 13, 1929; *Daily Press* (Newport News, VA), April 27, 1929; *Daily Press* (Newport News, VA), September 11, 1929; *Daily Press* (Newport News, VA), August 15, 1930; *Time* 17, no. 20 (May 18, 1931): 54.

21. *Pittsburgh Sun-Telegraph*, June 7, 1931; *Daily Press* (Newport News, VA), April 17, 1932; *Daily Press* (Newport News, VA), April 26, 1932; "Exercises at Cape Henry to Commemorate One Hundred and Fiftieth Anniversary of Lighthouse Service," *Coast Guard Bulletin* 1, no. 1 (July 1939): 3; "Celebration of One Hundred and Fiftieth Anniversary of Lighthouse Service a Marked Success," *Coast Guard Bulletin* 1, no. 2 (August 1939): 10; "Whale Oil and Wicks," *Mariners Weather Log* 32, no. 4 (Fall 1988): 23; Dolin, *Brilliant Beacons*, 230.

22. *Daily Press* (Newport News, VA), April 6, 1963; *Daily Press* (Newport News, VA), July 27, 1966; *Daily Press* (Newport News, VA), August 5, 1989; *Daily Press* (Newport News, VA), July 29, 1990; *Daily Press* (Newport News, VA), December 9, 1998; *Daily Press* (Newport News, VA), April 6, 2003; *Daily Press* (Newport News, VA), June 3, 2003; *Daily Press* (Newport News, VA), November 22, 2012; *Democrat and Chronicle* (Rochester, NY), January 20, 1999; *Evening Sun* (Hanover, PA), July 25, 1999; (Cocoa Beach) *Florida Today*, March 31, 2002.

23. *News Leader* (Staunton, VA), July 18, 2003; *News Leader* (Staunton, VA), October 7, 2011; *Baltimore Sun*, August 1, 2003.

24. "Preservation Virginia Reopens Cape Henry Lighthouse Tower for Public Climbing," *Keeper's Log* 35, no. 3 (Summer 2019): 38–39; "Old Cape Henry Lighthouse Reopens," *Keeper's Log* 37, no. 3 (Summer 2021): 40–42.

25. *Baltimore Sun*, February 7, 1878; *Baltimore Sun*, February 21, 1881; *Baltimore Sun*, February 23, 1881; *Raleigh News*, February 14, 1878; *Richmond Dispatch*, June 6, 1878; *Richmond Dispatch*, September 11, 1879; *News Journal* (Wilmington, DE), September 11, 1879; Dolin, *Brilliant Beacons*, 196.

26. Geoffrey Perret, *Ulysses S. Grant: Soldier & President* (New York: Random House, 1997), 441–42; *Baltimore Sun*, June 8, 1881; *National Republican* (Washington, D.C.), December 17, 1881.

27. *Boston Post*, November 28, 1881; *Baltimore Sun*, December 16, 1881; *National Republican* (Washington, D.C.), December 17, 1881; *Democratic Advocate* (Westminster, MD), November 6, 1886.

28. *Alexandria Gazette*, January 19, 1886; *Alexandria Gazette*, July 23, 1886; *Democratic Advocate* (Westminster, MD), November 6, 1886.

29. *Norfolk Virginian*, January 9, 1887; *Norfolk Virginian*, August 14, 1887.

30. *Norfolk Virginian*, November 26, 1887; *Norfolk Virginian*, November 27, 1887; *Norfolk Virginian*, December 25, 1887 (quotation); *Official Register of the United States, Containing a List of Officers and Employé in the Civil, Military, and Naval Service*, vol. 1 (Washington, D.C.: Government Printing Office, 1881), 219 (Hereinafter *ORP*, all citations in volume one.); *ORP* (1881),

219; *ORP* (1883), 246; *Baltimore Sun*, December 21, 1887; *Wilmington* (NC) *Morning Star*, December 21, 1887; *Richmond Dispatch*, January 7, 1888.

31. *Weekly Virginian and Carolinian* (Norfolk), December 1, 1887; *Evening Star* (Washington, D.C.), December 27, 1887; *Norfolk Virginian*, January 12, 1888; *Norfolk Virginian*, January 17, 1888; *Norfolk Virginian*, February 21, 1888; *Norfolk Virginian*, February 26, 1888; *Norfolk Virginian*, February 28, 1888.

32. Robert H. Burgess, ed., *Coasting Captain: Journals of Leonard S. Tawes* (Newport News, VA: The Mariners' Museum, 1967), 252–54 (quotation on 254); "Norfolk Harbor," *Our Navy* 12, no. 6 (October 1918), 64–65.

33. *Baltimore Sun*, October 17, 1896; *Baltimore Sun*, October 21, 1903; *Norfolk Virginian*, October 11, 1896; *Norfolk Virginian*, November 13, 1896 (quotation); *Norfolk Virginian*, March 12, 1897; *Evening Star* (Washington, D.C.) October 21, 1903; *Blue Book of American Shipping* (Cleveland, OH: Marine Review, 1900), 396.

34. *Baltimore City Directory* (Baltimore: R.L. Polk, 1893), 132 (Hereinafter *CD* for the cities of Baltimore, Norfolk and Newport News, various titles and publishers.); *CD-Baltimore* (1897), 140; *ORP* (1901), 354; *ORP* (1903), 1,132; *Evening Star* (Washington, D.C.), July 11, 1903; *Baltimore Sun*, November 13, 1903.

35. "443.-United States.-Virginia," *Nautical Magazine* 46, no. 12 (December 1880): 1,034; *AR-Treasury* (1893), 97; *Daily Press* (Newport News, VA), February 11, 1911; *Baltimore Sun*, February 11, 1911.

36. *Eleventh Annual Report of the Secretary of Commerce, 1923* (Washington, D.C., 1923), 49, 74 (Hereinafter, *AR-Commerce*.); "Visitors at Lighthouses," *Lighthouse Service Bulletin* 5, no. 40 (April 1939): 173.

37. *Asheville* (NC) *Gazette-News*, January 2, 1912; *Washington Times*, November 4, 1921; *Richmond Dispatch*, November 7, 1921; *Baltimore Sun*, July 12, 1922; *Baltimore Sun*, January 18, 1924; *Baltimore Sun*, May 4, 1924; *Buoy List: Cape Henlopen to Cape Lookout* (Washington, D.C.: Government Printing Office, 1926), 13 (Hereinafter *Buoy List*.).

38. George R. Putnam, "Radio Fog Signals for the Protection of Navigation: Recent Progress," *Proceedings of the National Academy of Sciences* 10, no. 6 (June 15, 1924): 211–18; *Hartford Courant*, November 29, 1925; *Baltimore Sun*, May 20, 1939.

39. Richard P. Weinert Jr. and Robert Arthur, *Defender of the Chesapeake: The Story of Fort Monroe*, 3rd rev. ed. (Shippensburg, PA: White Mane, 1989), 273–74; *Dayton Daily News*, November 13, 1936; *Daily Press* (Newport News, VA), December 29, 1932; *Daily Press* (Newport News, VA), June 20, 1938; *Evening Sun* (Baltimore), October 6, 1939.

40. Thomas A. Tag, "Testing of the Xenon Strobe Lamp System in America," *Keeper's Log*, 36, no. 4 (Fall 2020): 26.

41. *Daily Press* (Newport News, VA), December 16, 1981; *Daily Press* (Newport News, VA), December 2, 1983; *Star-Democrat* (Easton, MD), December 2, 1983.

42. *Hartford Courant*, November 3, 2000; Lighthouse Friends, "Cape Henry (New), VA," www.lighthousefriends.com.

Chapter 2

43. *Norfolk Virginian*, December 29, 1895.

44. Joan D. Charles, comp., *Hampton Ink, 1707–1922* (Hampton, VA: Joan Charles, 2009), 78; *National Intelligence and Washington Advertiser* (Washington, D.C.), October 17, 1804.

45. Dudley, *Naval War of 1812*, 2: 396–97; *Hartford Courant*, March 23, 1813; (Philadelphia) *Pennsylvania Gazette*, December 28, 1814.

46. Weinert and Arthur, *Defender of the Chesapeake*, 30.

47. John V. Quarstein and Julia Steere Clevenger, *Old Point Comfort Resort: Hospitality, Health and History on Virginia's Chesapeake Bay* (Charleston, SC: The History Press, 2009), 15–17.

48. Light-House Board, comp., *Laws of the United States Relating to the Establishment, Support, and Management of the Light-Houses…from August 7, 1789 to March 3, 1855* (Washington, D.C.: Government Printing Office, 1855), 107; *Report of the Officers Constituting the Light-House Board...1851* (Washington, D.C.: A.O.P. Nicholson, 1852), 187; *Baltimore Sun*, September 14, 1854.

49. Virginia Neal Thomas, "Women's Work: Female Lighthouse Keepers in the Early in the Early Republic, 1820–1859," unpublished thesis, Old Dominion University, 2010, 11, 37, 46, 50, 97; Mary Louise Clifford and J. Candace Clifford, *Women Who Kept the Lights: An Illustrated History of Female Lighthouse Keepers*, 2nd ed. (Williamsburg, VA: Cypress Communications, 1993), 1–3; Shona Riddell, *Guiding Lights: The Extraordinary Lives of Lighthouse Women* (Dunedin, NZ: Exisle, 2020), 73–104.

50. Find a Grave, "Amelia Dewees, Buried in St. John's Church Cemetery, Hampton, VA, FG Memorial 24914834," www.findagrave.com; Les Jensen, *32nd Virginia Infantry* (Lynchburg, VA: H.E. Howard, 1990), 181.

51. Larry Saint, et al., *Screwpiles: The Forgotten Lighthouses* (Brookfield, MO: Donning, 2018), 35–36; Weinert and Arthur, *Defender of the Chesapeake*, 158.

52. Weinert and Arthur, *Defender of the Chesapeake*, 106–7; *Daily Press* (Newport News, VA), April 29, 2018; *Richmond Dispatch*, May 14, 1869 (first quotation); *AR-Treasury* (1869), 201 (second quotation); Robert Knox Sneden, *Eye of the Storm: A Civil War Odyssey*, edited by Charles F. Bryan Jr. and Nelson D. Lankford (New York: Free Press, 2000), 29 (third quotation).

53. *AR-Light House Board* (1886), 48; Phyllis Sprock, comp., copy of Department of the Army, Inventory of Historic Property form, Fort Monroe, VA, building 60 (67 Fenwick Road), 1980, in possession of the author.

54. Robert Francis Engs, *Freedom's First Generation: Black Hampton, Virginia, 1861–1890* (Philadelphia, PA: University of Pennsylvania Press, 1970), 16–17, 52, 92–93; *ORP* (1881), 219; *Evening Star* (Washington, D.C.), January 30, 1908.

55. Joan Charles, comp., *Elizabeth City County, Virginia African American Census Records, 1850, 1860, 1870* (Hampton, VA: Joan Charles, 1999), 40; A.P. Davis, "William Roscoe Davis and His Descendants," *Negro History Bulletin* 13, no. 4 (January 1950): 81–82; Engs, *Freedom's First Generation*, 16–17, 52, 92–93; *ORP* (1873), 162; *Norfolk Landmark*, October 15, 1878.

56. *Evening Star* (Washington, D.C.), January 30, 1908; *Norfolk Virginian*, September 4, 1878; Clunies, "African American Lighthouse Keepers," 11.

57. George Dewey to the secretary of the treasury, October 16, 1880, box 5, J-K, Correspondence Concerning Keepers and Assistants, 1821–1902, NC-31, entry 82, RG 26, Records of the U.S. Coast Guard, NARA.

58. Leonard, *General Assembly*, 525; Clunies, "African American Lighthouse Keepers," 11; Ancestry, "Sallie T. Jones, U.S. Census of 1900, Elizabeth City County, VA," www.ancestry.com.

59. R.D. Evans to chairman of the Light-House Board, November 12, 1885, box 5, J-K, Correspondence Concerning Keepers and Assistants, 1821–1902, NC-31, entry 82, RG 26, Records of the U.S. Coast Guard, NARA; R.D. Evans to Lawrence S. Babbitt, October 5, 1885, box 5, J-K, Correspondence Concerning Keepers and Assistants, 1821–1902, NC-31, entry 82, RG 26, Records of the U.S. Coast Guard, NARA; *Richmond Dispatch*, November 13, 1877; *Baltimore Sun*, March 3, 1881; *ORP* (1881), 219.

60. *AR-Treasury* (1886), 138; *Home Bulletin, Soldiers Home* (Hampton, VA), September 4, 1886.

61. *Evening Star* (Washington, D.C.), January 30, 1908; *Daily Press* (Newport News, VA), January 25, 1908; *Washington Bee*, February 8, 1908.

62. Ancestry, "VA Certificate of Death, no. 19541, for Elijah Albert Hozier, September 3, 1918," www.ancestry.com; *Evening Star* (Washington, D.C.), December 14, 1916; *Evening Star* (Washington, D.C.), February 19,

1917; *Baltimore Sun*, October 14, 1921; *Daily Press* (Newport News, VA), September 1, 1918.

63. "Marking of Lighthouse Roofs for Seaplanes, Chesapeake Bay," *Lighthouse Service Bulletin* 3, no. 29 (May 1, 1926): 135.

64. "Lightbeam [*sic*] Control Fog Signals," *Lighthouse Service Bulletin* 5, no. 14 (February 1937): 56.

65. *Daily Press* (Newport News, VA), June 6, 1937; *Daily Press* (Newport News, VA), June 22, 1941; "Visitors to Lighthouses," *Lighthouse Service Bulletin* 5, no. 40 (April 1, 1939): 173.

66. Quarstein and Clevenger, *Point Comfort Resort*, 78; Weinert and Arthur, *Defender of the Chesapeake*, 273–75; *Indianapolis News*, May 21, 1941; *Daily Press* (Newport News, VA), March 21, 1941; *Daily Press* (Newport News, VA), January 4, 1942; *Daily Press* (Newport News, VA), November 18, 1945; *Evening Sun* (Baltimore), June 9, 1945.

67. "Lighthouses Are Again Open to Visitors," *Coast Guard Bulletin* 3, no. 22 (April 1947): 341; *Times-Herald* (Newport News, VA), December 1, 1957.

68. Linda Turbyville, *Bay Beacons: Lighthouses of the Chesapeake Bay* (Annapolis, MD: Eastwind, 1995), 112; Clifford, *Historic Light Stations*, 319 (This source has 1972 as the automation date.); *Daily Press* (Newport News, VA), November 18, 1945; *Daily Press* (Newport News, VA), November 15, 1953; *Daily Press* (Newport News, VA), March 27, 1960; *Daily Press* (Newport News, VA), September 11, 1960; *Daily Press* (Newport News, VA), July 15, 1963; *Daily Press* (Newport News, VA), October 27, 1969; *Cincinnati Enquirer*, December 19, 1953; *Tallahassee Democrat*, March 24, 1972.

69. Weinert and Arthur, *Defender of the Chesapeake*, 178; Haunted Places, "The Chamberlin," https://www.hauntedplaces.org/item/the-chamberlin/; Jane K. Polonsky and Joan M. Drum, *A Galaxy of Ghosts* (Hampton, VA: Polyndrum, 1992), 35; L.B. Taylor Jr., *Ghosts of Tidewater* (Williamsburg, VA: L.B. Taylor, 1990), 89–96.

70. *Daily Press* (Newport News, VA), November 21, 1999; *Daily Press* (Newport News, VA), May 21, 2002; interview with Barbara G. Bauer, conducted by Benjamin H. Trask, June 25, 2020; phone interviews with Barbara G. Bauer, conducted by Benjamin H. Trask, March 10, 2020, and January 26, 2023.

71. Bauer interview with Trask, June 25, 2020; Bauer phone interview with Trask, March 10, 2020; *Daily Press* (Newport News, VA), December 24, 2015.

72. *Daily Press* (Newport News, VA), August 27, 1972.

73. *Daily Press* (Newport News, VA), February 22, 1909; *Daily Press* (Newport News, VA), March 29, 2020.

Chapter 3

74. Herman Böÿe, "Map of the State of Virginia (corrected 1859)," in *A Description of the Country: Virginia's Cartographers and Their Maps, 1607–1881*, edited by E.M. Sanchez-Saavedra (Richmond: Virginia State Library, 1975), maps; Charles, *Hampton Ink*, 162.

75. Parramore, *Norfolk*, 137; *ORP* (1829), 58; *American Beacon* (Norfolk, VA), June 18, 1829.

76. *American Beacon* (Norfolk, VA), June 18, 1829.

77. Wayne Wheeler, "Winslow Lewis: A Nineteenth-Century Lighthouse Scalawag," *Keeper's Log* 21, no. 4 (Summer 2005): 18–24; Thomas Gordon, comp., *A Collection of the Laws of the United States Relating to Revenue, Navigation and Commerce and Light-Houses & c up to March 4, 1843* (Philadelphia, PA: Isaac Ashmead, 1844), 939; Levitt, *Short, Bright Flash*, 135.

78. Francis Ross Holland Jr., *America's Lighthouses: Their Illustrated History Since 1716* (Brattleboro, VT: S. Greene, 1972), 14–17; Levitt, *Short, Bright Flash*, 139, 144; Ray Jones, *Lighthouse Encyclopedia* (Guilford, CT: Globe Pequot, n.p.), 23–28; Lewis Updyke, "Winslow Lewis and the Lighthouses," *American Neptune* 28, no. 1 (January 1968), 46–48. Updyke is one of the few supporters of Winslow Lewis's practices.

79. *American Beacon* (Norfolk, VA), June 18, 1829; Updyke, "Winslow Lewis," 44.

80. Charles F. Elliot, *Fox Hill: Its People and Places* (Hampton, VA: Charles F. Elliot, 1976), 8–9.

81. Alexander Crosby Brown, *Steam Packets on the Chesapeake: A History of the Old Bay Line, Since 1840* (Cambridge, MD: Tidewater, 1961), 11–12; Joan Charles, comp., *Virginia and Maryland Shipwreck Accounts, 1623 to 1950* (Hampton, VA: Joan Charles, 2004), passim.

82. *Report of Light-House Board*, 1852, 187.

83. Ibid., 186 (quotation); *Population Schedules of the Seventh Census of the United States*, 1850, Virginia (slave schedules) Cumberland-Fluvanna Counties, roll 986, microcopy no. 432, NARA, 1964.

84. Charles Elliott, "Back River Lighthouse," *Keeper's Log* 9, no. 2 (Winter 1995): 21; *Richmond Dispatch*, September 3, 1859 (quote); *Daily Exchange* (Baltimore, MD), August 23, 1859; *Baltimore Sun*, August 25, 1859; *AR-Treasury* (1855), 261; *AR-Lighthouse Board* (1855), 412–13.

85. Weinert and Arthur, *Defender of the Chesapeake*, 94–97; *Official Records of the Union and Confederate Navies in the War of the Rebellion*, 40 vols., first series (Washington, D.C., 1894–1912), 5:371, 723 (Hereinafter *ORN* first series unless otherwise stated.).

86. *ORN*, 6:74 (quotation); Louis R. Manarin, comp., *North Carolina Troops, 1861–1865: A Roster*, vol. 3 (Raleigh, NC: NC Office of Archives and History, 2004), 1–2.
87. *Charleston* (SC) *Courier*, September 11, 1861.
88. *New York Herald*, April 16, 186; *ACP* (1863), 343.
89. *Daily Morning Chronicle* (Washington, D.C.), May 23, 1867.
90. Martha W. McCartney, *Mathews County Virginia: Lost Landscapes, Untold Stories* (Mathews, VA: Mathews Historical Society, 2015), 401; Charles, *Hampton Ink*, 167, 176; Clunies, "African American Lighthouse Keepers," 9, 11.
91. Mary F. Armstrong and Helen W. Ludlow, *Hampton and Its Students by Two of Its Teachers* (New York: G.P. Putnam's Sons, 1874), 121; Robert Francis Engs, *Educating the Disfranchised and Disinherited: Samuel Chapman Armstrong and Hampton Institute, 1839–1893* (Knoxville: University of Tennessee Press, 1999), 64; Engs, *Freedom's First Generation*, 16, 52, 91–93.
92. *ORP* (1873), 204; *Daily Press* (Newport News, VA), May 14, 1909.
93. *ORP* (1873), 204.
94. "Stone Rip-Raps for Back River Light Station," *Sanitary Engineer and Construction Record* 16, no. 10 (August 6, 1887): 271; *Baltimore Sun*, April 30, 1885; *AR-Treasury* (1888), 81.
95. *Report of the Superintendent of the Survey During the Year, 1866*, Washington, D.C., 1869, 17; *AR-Navy*, 1884, i, 94 (quotation).
96. Charles, *Shipwreck Accounts*, 162; *Daily Press* (Newport News, VA), October 7, 1905.
97. U.S. States Commission of Fish and Fisheries, *Report of the Commission of 1887* (Washington, D.C., Government Printing Office, 1891), 568; Bureau of Fisheries, *Statistics of the Fisheries of the Middle Atlantic States for 1904* (Washington, D.C.: Government Printing Office, 1907), 100; *Hampton* (VA) *Monitor*, January 30, 1913 (corrected to 1914); Elliot, *Fox Hill*, 47–60; *Evening Star* (Washington, D.C.), April 29, 1908; *Daily Press* (Newport News, VA), March 3, 1915.
98. *Baltimore Sun*, December 9, 1904.
99. *Baltimore Sun*, September 7, 1909; *Mathews Journal*, September 9, 1909; *Daily Press* (Newport News, VA), July 30, 1914.
100. Patrick Hornberger and Linda Turbyville, *Forgotten Beacons: The Lost Lighthouses of the Chesapeake Bay* (Annapolis, MD: Eastwind, 1997), 18; *Daily Press* (Newport News, VA), July 7, 1985; Earl W. Thomson, "La Premiere," *Liaison: The Courier of the Big Gun Corps* 3, no. 9 (February 28, 1920): 109; *Evening Sun* (Baltimore, MD), April 6, 1915.

101. Douglas B. Hague and Rosemary Christie, *Lighthouses: Their Architecture, History and Archaeology* (Llandysul, UK: Gomer, 1975), 157–59; Dolin, *Brilliant Beacons*, 192–93.

102. Ann Davis, *Down by the Back River Light* (New York: Morgan James, 2006), passim; Nancy E. Sheppard, *Hampton Roads: Murder & Mayhem* (Charleston, SC: The History Press, 2018), 93–95; Park Rouse Jr., *The Good Old Days in Hampton and Newport News* (Richmond, VA: Dietz Press, 1986), 203–4; *Daily Press* (Newport News, VA), February 6, 1898; *Daily Press* (Newport News, VA), September 12, 1931.

103. Ancestry, "VA Certificate of Death, No. 27976 for Jenny Graham Kane, Sept. 12, 1931," www.ancestory.com; Rouse, *Good Old Days*, 203–4; *Daily Press* (Newport News, VA), September 12, 1931.

104. Rouse, *Good Old Days*, 205–6.

105. *News-Herald* (Franklin, PA), September 18, 1931; *Washington Herald*, September 15, 1931.

106. *Times-Herald* (Newport News, VA), December 12, 1931; *Daily Press* (Newport News, VA), December 10, 1931, *Daily Press* (Newport News, VA), December 11, 1931.

107. *Daily Press* (Newport News, VA), December 10, 1931.

108. Percy Carmel, comp., Kane murder trail clipping volumes, 1931–32 and partial transcript of *Commonwealth of Virginia v. Elisha Kent Kane* in the Justice Court of Elizabeth City County, Virginia, September 30, 1931, vol. 9, 92 (second quotation), 94 (fourth and fifth quotation), 95 (third quotation), 96–97 (first quotation), Virginiana Room, Hampton Public Library; *Evening Star* (Washington, D.C.), December 9, 1931.

109. Rouse, *Good Old Days*, 204–5.

110. *Daily Press* (Newport News, VA), August 24, 1933; *Daily Press* (Newport News, VA), February 1, 1938; *Daily Press* (Newport News, VA), September 24, 2014.

111. *Daily Press* (Newport News, VA), August 11, 1940.

112. Interview with Diane Nickerson Tingen, conducted by B.H. Trask, Hampton, VA, November 17, 2018; interview with Robert C. Deal, conducted by B.H. Trask, Hampton, VA, November 25, 2021; *Daily Press* (Newport News, VA), July 4, 1949.

113. *Daily Press* (Newport News, VA), September 27, 1956.

114. *Times-Herald* (Newport News, VA), June 14, 1972; *Daily Press* (Newport News, VA), April 25, 1973; *Daily Press* (Newport News, VA), February 27, 1987.

Chapter 4

115. *New York Daily Herald*, May 19, 1847; *Morning Chronicle* (London), June 16, 1847; *Southern Weekly Post* (Raleigh, NC), July 9, 1853; *Daily Republic* (Washington, D.C.), October 5, 1850; *Union* (Washington, D.C.), August 5, 1853.

116. Saint, *Screwpiles*, 54–61; Hague and Christie, *Lighthouse Archeology*, 136–37; Noble, *Lighthouses & Keepers*, 43.

117. *Union* (Washington, D.C.), August 5, 1853; *AR-Treasury* (1856), 356; *Evening Star* (Washington, D.C.), September 4, 1854.

118. Levitt, *Short, Bright Flash*, 210; *AR-Treasury* (1858), 245; Hornberger and Turbyville, *Forgotten Beacons*, 43.

119. *Daily News* (London), February 6, 1862; *ORN* 11:90, 97; *AR-Treasury* (1863), 150; *AR-Treasury* (1865), 195; *List of Light-Houses, Lighted Beacons and Floating Lights of the Atlantic, Gulf, and Pacific Coasts of the United States* (Washington, D.C.: Government Printing Office, 1865), 40 (Hereinafter *Light List.*); *Alexandria Gazette*, May 16, 1866.

120. "The Light-House Board Have Issued the Following Notices to Mariners," *Army and Navy Journal* 4, no. 25 (February 9, 1867): 394; *Norfolk Virginian*, January 17, 1867; *Richmond Dispatch*, February 1, 1867.

121. *National Republican* (Washington, D.C.), February 25, 1867; *National Republican* (Washington, D.C.), November 12, 1867; *Richmond Dispatch*, April 30, 1867; *Richmond Dispatch*, May 18, 1867; *Richmond Dispatch*, November 2, 1867; *Baltimore Sun*, December 28, 1867.

122. *Alexandria Gazette*, July 6, 1881 (first quotation); *Alexandria Gazette*, May 30, 1885 (second and third quotation); *ORP* (1875), 196; *ORP* (1879), 196; *ORP* (1885), 221; *Richmond Dispatch*, July 25, 1885; Jane Dailey, *Before Jim Crow: The Politics of Race in Postemancipation Virginia* (Chapel Hill: University of North Carolina Press, 2000), 157–58; James T. Moore, *Two Paths to the New South: The Virginia Debt Controversy, 1870–1883* (Lexington: University of Kentucky Press, 2014), 385.

123. Letter from the secretary of the treasury transmitting estimates of appropriations required for the service of the fiscal year ending June 30, 1895, Washington, D.C.: Government Printing, 1893 [*sic*], 317, appendix; *Baltimore Sun*, December 1, 1890; *Norfolk Virginian*, January 3, 1896; *Light List* (1907), 136.

124. *Baltimore Sun*, June 1, 1900; *Baltimore Sun*, July 3, 1900; *Baltimore Sun*, August 24, 1902; *Baltimore Sun*, April 19, 1907; *Baltimore Sun*, August 26, 1928; *Evening Star* (Washington, D.C.), July 23, 1902; *Evening Star* (Washington, D.C.), August 27, 1906.

125. Taylor, *Ghosts of Tidewater*, 1–4.

126. *Notice to Mariners*, no. 3 (January 19, 1918): 72–73 (first quotation); "Saving of Life and Property," *Lighthouse Service Bulletin* 2, no. 10 (October 1, 1918): 43 (second quotation).

127. *Daily Press* (Newport News, VA), February 26, 1927; *Daily Press* (Newport News, VA), July 8, 1932; *Boston Globe*, July 20, 1932.

128. *Baltimore Sun*, January 21, 1931; *Daily Press* (Newport News, VA), February 19, 1931 (quotation).

129. *Daily Press* (Newport News, VA), February 16, 1936; *Daily Press* (Newport News, VA), February 2, 1940; *Daily Press* (Newport News, VA), February 10, 1940 (quotation).

130. *Daily Press* (Newport News, VA), May 7, 1941.

131. *Daily Press* (Newport News, VA), October 25, 1949; *Daily Press* (Newport News, VA), September 20, 1953 (quotation); *Daily Press* (Newport News, VA), April 22, 1954; *Daily Press* (Newport News), October 20, 1963; *Daily Press* (Newport News, VA), March 15, 1964; *Daily Press* (Newport News, VA), January 24, 1965; U.S. Department of Transportation, Maritime Administration, "James River Reserve Fleet," https://www.maritime.dot.gov/history/vessels-maritime-administration/james-river-reserve-fleet; Robert de Gast, *Lighthouses of the Chesapeake* (Baltimore, MD: Johns Hopkins University Press, 1973), 150; Lighthouse Friends, "Deep Water Shoals, VA," www.lighthousefriends.com.

Chapter 5

132. *Union* (Washington, D.C.), August 5, 1853; *Evening Star* (Washington, D.C.), September 4, 1854; *AR-Treasury* (1856), 356, 360.

133. Robert J. Driver Jr., *5th Virginia Cavalry* (Lynchburg, VA: H.E. Howard, 1997), 158; *Light List* (1865), 40; *Daily News* (London), February 6, 1862; *Annual Report of the Secretary of War* 2, no. 1 (1882): 889 (Hereinafter *AR-War.*); *AR-Treasury* (1863), 150; *AR-Treasury* (1865), 195.

134. *Log of William F. Martin*, 1869–1870 (40380), November [December] 27, 1869–January 2, 1870, United States Bureau of Lighthouses, Fifth Lighthouse District, Library of Virginia, Richmond, VA; *AR-Treasury* (1869), 448; de Gast, *Lighthouses*, 149.

135. *Richmond News Leader*, February 1, 1868; *Alexandria Gazette*, February 29, 1868.

136. *AR-Treasury* (1869), 447; Peter C. Harris to Admiral [W.B. Shurbrick], June 12, 1871, letterbook 274, box 172, entry 24, RG 26, Suffolk Heritage River Collection, https://archives.uslhs.org/about-lighthouse-research-catalog.
137. *Norfolk Virginian*, June 1, 1871 (quotation); *Norfolk Virginian*, June 17, 1871; *AR-Treasury* (1869), 447–48.
138. *Norfolk Virginian*, June 17, 1871.
139. *AR-War* 2, no. 1 (1882): 889.
140. Moore, *Two Paths*, 385; *Valley Virginian* (Stanton), April 22, 1880; *Norfolk Virginian*, September 29, 1881; *Norfolk Landmark*, August 24, 1889; *Daily Press* (Newport News, VA), August 16, 1964.
141. *Buoy List* (1923), 58; *Light List* (1907), 137.
142. *Light List* (1907), 136.

Chapter 6

143. *Light List* (1865), 40; *Tri-Weekly Commercial* (Wilmington, NC), September 21, 1852; *Union* (Washington, D.C.), August 5, 1853; *Evening Star* (Washington, D.C.), September 4, 1854; *AR-War* 2, no. 1 (1882): 889.
144. *AR-Treasury* (1856), 356 (first quotation); *Daily News* (London), February 6, 1862 (second quotation); *AR-Treasury* (1863), 150; *AR-Treasury* (1865), 195.
145. Hornberger and Turbyville, *Forgotten Beacons*, 43; *AR-Treasury* (1869), 447.
146. Clunies, "African American Lighthouse Keepers," 9; *Baltimore Sun*, November 8, 1881; *Richmond Dispatch*, July 25, 1885; *ORP* (1881), 219.
147. *Daily Press* (Newport News, VA), March 20, 1907; *Washington Post*, March 20, 1907; *Leader-Post* (Regina, Saskatchewan, CA), March 28, 1907. Note that Simonsen's name appeared as "Fimerson" in these articles.
148. *Light List* (1907), 136; *Daily Press* (Newport News, VA), August 24, 1911.
149. *Times-Dispatch* (Richmond, VA), April 4, 1918; *Notice to Mariners*, no. 3 (January 19, 1918): 72–73 (quotation on 73).
150. *Daily Press* (Newport News, VA), May 10, 1931.
151. Ibid.
152. *Daily Press* (Newport News, VA), February 18, 1979; *Daily Press* (Newport News, VA), October 22, 1979; *Daily Press* (Newport News, VA), May 3, 1988; Hornberger and Turbyville, *Forgotten Beacons*, 43; de Gast, *Lighthouses*, 23.

Chapter 7

153. James Delgado, "The Development of the American Lightship," *Keeper's Log* 6, no. 2 (Winter 1990): 2–12.

154. *ACP* (1822), 219; *ACP* (1827), 115; *Alexandria Gazette*, September 1, 1859; *Evening Post* (New York), June 11, 1831; Hornberger and Turbyville, *Forgotten Beacons*, 28.

155. Parramore, *Norfolk*, 144–45; William C. Wooldridge, *Mapping Virginia* (Charlottesville: University Press of Virginia, 2012), 245.

156. *National Gazette* (Philadelphia, PA), August 3, 1827 (first quotation); *New York Times*, January 16, 1855 (second quotation); Peggy Haile McPhillips and Benjamin H. Trask, "The Darker Side of Commerce: Yellow Fever and the Chesapeake Bay," *Chesapeake Bay Maritime Museum Quarterly* 1, no. 4 (Winter 2003–4): 13–17; *Virginian-Pilot* (Norfolk, VA), January 27, 1900.

157. *Vermont Gazette* (Bennington), June 29, 1824; *Report of Light-House Board*, 1852, 183.

158. *Argus* (Norfolk, VA), January 20, 1857 (first quotation); *Richmond Dispatch*, January 26, 1857; *Richmond Dispatch*, February 2, 1857; *Richmond Dispatch*, February 6, 1857 (second quotation); *Baltimore Sun*, February 6, 1857; H.W. Burton, *The History of Norfolk, Virginia* (Norfolk, VA: Norfolk Virginian Job Print, 1877), 27–28.

159. "The Memorial of Washington Allon Barlett, Late A Lieutenant in the Navy" (Washington, D.C.: G.S. Gideon, 1856), 5; Noble, *Lighthouse & Keepers*, 22–26; Levitt, *Short, Bright Flash*, 165–68; *Daily Republic* (Washington, D.C.), April 26, 1852; *New York Daily Herald*, February 12, 1855.

160. *Baltimore Sun*, August 31, 1859; *Baltimore Sun*, November 5, 1859; *Alexandria Gazette*, September 1, 1859; *Daily Journal* (Wilmington, NC), November 5, 1859; *CD-Norfolk*, 1859, 53.

161. Donald G. Shomette, *Shipwrecks on the Chesapeake: Maritime Disasters on Chesapeake Bay and Its Tributaries, 1608–1978* (Centreville, MD: Tidewater, 1982), 119; Benjamin H. Trask, *9th Virginia Infantry* (Lynchburg, VA: H.E. Howard, 1984), 3–4; *ORN* 6:740–41.

162. Thomas O. Selfridge Jr., "The Merrimac and the Cumberland," *Cosmopolitan* 15, no. 2 (June 1893): 181.

163. Ibid.; Saint, *Screwpiles*, 37 (This source suggests the blast may have destroyed the lighthouse in May 1862.); *ORN* 7:337.

164. Saint, *Screwpiles*, 41; *ACP* (1863), 341.

165. Clifford and Clifford, *Women Who Kept the Lights*, 2.

166. *ORP* (1871), 78.

167. *AR-Treasury* (1880), 35; *AR-Treasury* (1883), 25, 297; *Baltimore Sun*, August 18, 1883.

168. Janet B. Hewett, ed., *The Roster of Union Soldiers, 1861–1865: United States Colored Troops*, vol. 2 (Wilmington, NC: Broadfoot, 1997), 220; Dailey, *Before Jim Crow*, 57 (quotation), 67; *Richmond Dispatch*, May 20, 1879; *Baltimore Sun*, April 20, 1881; *Baltimore Sun*, November 2, 1882.

169. Parramore, *Norfolk*, 271–74; *Daily Press* (Newport News, VA), April 21, 1932; *Baltimore Sun*, February 17, 1907.

170. *Evening Star* (Washington, D.C.), December 22, 1906; *Baltimore Sun*, January 17, 1907; *Baltimore Sun*, June 3, 1911 (quotation); *Daily Press* (Newport News, VA), December 8, 1949.

171. *Virginian-Pilot* (Norfolk, VA), October 15, 1907; *Washington Times*, June 4, 1915.

172. *Tampa* (FL) *Times*, July 9, 1914 (first quotation); *Evening Star* (Washington, D.C.), June 5, 1915 (second quotation); *AR-Commerce* (1915), 66.

173. *Baltimore Sun*, May 26, 1919; *Baltimore Sun*, July 11, 1919; *Baltimore Sun*, August 26, 1919; *1925 Annual, Hampton Roads Maritime Exchange* (Norfolk, VA: Hampton Roads Maritime Exchange, 1925), 8; Board of Engineers for Rivers and Harbors, comp., *The Ports of Norfolk, Portsmouth, Newport News and Hampton, Va.* (Washington, D.C.: Government Printing Office, 1935), passim.

174. Holland, *America's Lighthouses*, 49–50; "Food Products Raised by Lighthouse Keeper," *Lighthouse Service Bulletin* 2, no. 12 (December 2, 1918): 54 (quotation).

175. *AR-Commerce* (1919), 60; *AR-Commerce* (1922), 54; "Saving of Life and Property," *Lighthouse Service Bulletin* 2, no. 42 (June 1, 1922): 231.

176. *Applications and Papers towards Awarding of Medals: C.A. Sterling*, folder 181, box 289, RG 26, entry 283A, Records of the U.S. Coast Guard, NARA.

177. *Virginian-Pilot* (Norfolk, VA), July 27, 1924.

178. *News-Press* (Fort Myers, FL), November 7, 1930; *AR-Commerce* (1925), 8.

179. "Memo to Commandant, April 12, 1928," *Applications and Papers towards Awarding of Medals: C.A. Sterling*, folder 181, box 289, RG 26, entry 283A, Records of the U.S. Coast Guard, NARA; *AR-Commissioner of Lighthouses* (1928), 10; *Virginian-Pilot* (Norfolk, VA), December 30, 1927; *Lighthouse Service Bulletin* 3, no. 50 (February 1, 1928): 231–32.

180. *AR-Commerce* (1928), 10; *Daily Press* (Newport News, VA), January 27, 1932; *Daily Press* (Newport News, VA), November 8, 1933.

181. *AR-Commerce* (1928), 10; *Daily Press* (Newport News, VA), January 27, 1932.

Chapter 8

182. de Gast, *Lighthouses*, 148; *Daily State Journal* (Alexandria, VA), October 3, 1872; *Alexandria Gazette*, August 17, 1874; *Baltimore Sun*, January 17, 1871; *Norfolk* (VA) *Landmark*, August 8, 1900; *Daily Press* (Newport News, VA), December 13, 1957.

183. Bob Trapani Jr., *Lighthouses of Maryland and Virginia: History, Mystery, Legends and Love* (Elkton, MD: Myst and Lace, 2006), 63–65; *Norfolk Virginian*, June 30, 1873; McPhillips and Trask, "Darker Side of Commerce," 13–17.

184. *Norfolk Virginian*, December 20, 1876; *Richmond Dispatch*, May 24, 1877; *Norfolk* (VA) *Landmark*, October 31, 1878.

185. *Norfolk* (VA) *Landmark*, June 26, 1880; *Norfolk* (VA) *Landmark*, June 29, 1880.

186. *Baltimore Sun*, June 11, 1883; *Baltimore Sun*, November 21, 1884; *Baltimore Sun*, April 1, 1887; Parramore, *Norfolk*, 249–50.

187. *Norfolk* (VA) *Landmark*, August 12, 1887; *Virginian-Pilot* (Norfolk), October 14, 1899; *Baltimore Sun*, October 14, 1899; *Times* (Richmond, VA), December 22, 1892; *Evening Star* (Washington, DC), December 5, 1893; de Gast, *Lighthouses*, 148; *AR-Treasury* (1893), 90.

188. *Baltimore Sun*, January 18, 1924; "Lambert Point Fog Bell," *Lighthouse Service Bulletin* 3, no. 3 (March 1, 1924): 14.

189. Hornberger and Turbyville, *Forgotten Beacons*, 70; *Daily Press* (Newport News, VA), December 13, 1957.

Chapter 9

190. David Pickering, *The Cassell Dictionary of Folklore* (London: Cassell, 1999), 51, 111, 256–58, 287; *ACP* (1822), 219.

191. *ACP* (1863), 342; *ACP* (1867), 342 (quotation).

192. *Alexandria Gazette*, October 23, 1872; *AR-Treasury* (1880), 35; *Richmond Dispatch*, October 31, 1880; Jones, *Lighthouse Encyclopedia*, 125.

193. *Richmond Dispatch*, October 31, 1880; *Baltimore Sun*, November 18, 1880; *Baltimore Sun*, December 18, 1880.

194. *AR-Treasury* (1886), 138.

195. Clunies, "African American Lighthouse Keepers," 9, 11; *News and Observer* (Raleigh, NC), July 20, 1884.

196. Daily, *Before Jim Crow*, 63–64.

197. James N. Gregory to secretary of the treasury, July 11, 1889; *Correspondence Concerning Keepers and Assistants, 1821–1902*, box 8 D-Fo, NC 31, entry 82,

RG 26, U.S. Coast Guard Records, NARA; *Alexandria Gazette*, February 17, 1891; *Norfolk Virginian*, December 29, 1895.

198. *Virginian-Pilot* (Norfolk), December 17, 1907; *Daily Press* (Newport News, VA), December 17, 1907.

199. *Virginian-Pilot* (Norfolk), January 28, 1908.

200. *Virginian-Pilot* (Norfolk), January 28, 1908; *Daily Press* (Newport News, VA), January 28, 1908; *Mathews* (VA) *Journal*, February 13, 1908.

201. *Virginian-Pilot* (Norfolk), March 7, 1908; *Hawaiian Star* (Honolulu), March 17, 1908; *Daily Capital Journal* (Salem, OR), March 7, 1908.

202. *Daily Press* (Newport News, VA), December 29, 1909, as originally reported in the *Baltimore American*; *Evening Star* (Washington, D.C.), December 28, 1909.

203. *Daily Press* (Newport News, VA), December 28, 1909; *Evening Star* (Washington, D.C.), December 30, 1909.

204. *Evening Star* (Washington, D.C.), December 28, 1909; *Evening Star* (Washington, D.C.), December 30, 1909; *Evening Star* (Washington, D.C.), January 23, 1910; *Evening Star* (Washington, D.C.), February 14, 1910; *Daily Press* (Newport News, VA), December 29, 1909; *Daily Press* (Newport News, VA), February 2, 1910; *Baltimore Sun*, January 12, 1910.

205. *Hampton Monitor*, January 2, 1913 [*sic*], and *Daily Press* (Newport News, VA), January 3, 1914, refer to "Frank M. Cabell." However, the Find-A-Grave (memorial no. 5973391) gives the name "Ivanhoe Cabell." He was buried in Riverside Memorial Park in Norfolk, per an obituary found on findagrave.com.

206. Clifford, *Historic Light Stations*, 321.

207. Gregory J. Hansard, *German Sailors in Hampton Roads: A World War I Story at the Norfolk Navy Yard* (Charleston, SC: The History Press, 2018), 22–28; Parramore, *Norfolk*, 288–90; *Daily Press* (Newport News, VA), August 2, 1916; *Evening Star* (Washington, D.C.), May 27, 1917; Weinert and Arthur, *Defender of the Chesapeake*, 222.

208. "Saving of Life and Property," *Lighthouse Service Bulletin* 2, no. 9 (September 3, 1918): 40; "Efficiency Flags," *Lighthouse Service Bulletin* 2, no. 18 (June 2, 1919): 78.

209. "Saving of Life and Property," *Lighthouse Service Bulletin* 2, no. 41 (May 2, 1921): 180; "Saving of Life and Property," *Lighthouse Service Bulletin* 2, no. 48 (December 1, 1921): 208; "Saving of Life and Property," *Lighthouse Service Bulletin* 2, no. 68 (August 1, 1923): 292; "Saving of Life and Property," *Lighthouse Service Bulletin* 3, no. 1 (January 1, 1924): 6; "Saving of Life and Property," *Lighthouse Service Bulletin* 3, no. 47 (November 1,

1927): 220; "Saving of Life and Property," *Lighthouse Service Bulletin* 3, no. 36 (December 1, 1926): 167.

210. Weinert and Arthur, *Defender of the Chesapeake*, 272–88; Rouse, *Good Old Days*, 215–19; *Evening Sun* (Baltimore, MD), June 9, 1945.

211. Malcolm Muir Jr., "Hard Aground on Thimble Shoal," *Naval History* 5, no. 3 (Fall 1991): passim.

212. *Tampa* (FL) *Times*, February 2, 1950; *Daily Press* (Newport News, VA), January 18, 1951; *Daily Press* (Newport News, VA), January 19, 1951.

213. Paul Stillwell, *Battleship* Missouri: *An Illustrated History* (Annapolis, MD: Naval Institute Press, 1996), 145–64.

214. *Virginian-Pilot* (Norfolk, VA), October 13, 1961; *Ledger-Star* (Norfolk, VA), October 7, 1964; Clifford, *Historic Light Stations*, 321.

215. *Ledger-Star* (Norfolk, VA), September 20, 1988; *Virginian-Pilot* (Norfolk, VA), September 21, 1988; Dolin, *Brilliant Beacons*, 410; *Wall Street Journal*, August 15, 2013.

Chapter 10

216. J.A. Mowris, *A History of the One Hundred and Seventeenth Regiment, N.Y. Volunteers, (Fourth Oneida) from the Date of Its Organization, August 1862, Till That of Its Muster Out, June 1865* (Hartford, CT: Case, Lockwood, 1866), 64; *Baltimore* (MD) *Daily Commercial*, March 6, 1866; *Report of the Commissioner of Agriculture for the Year 1868*, Washington, D.C.: Government Printing Office, 1869, 343.

217. Saint, *Screwpiles*, 46–47; Hornberger and Turbyville, *Forgotten Beacons*, 78; *Light List* (1907), 136; *Baltimore Sun*, September 20, 1907.

218. *Daily State Journal* (Alexandria, VA), March 14, 1873; *Weekly Virginian and Carolinian* (Norfolk), August 28, 1884; *Norfolk Virginian*, August 26, 1888; *Norfolk Virginian*, August 23, 1898; *Norfolk Virginian*, August 21, 1902; Clunies, "African American Lighthouse Keepers," 8–11; *Baltimore Sun*, February 22, 1881; *Baltimore Sun*, July 13, 1889; *ORP* (1881), 219.

219. L.B. Hunley to J. Gilmore [*sic*] Hudgins, January 23, 1896, Hudgins family of Mathews, VA, scrapbook and papers, in possession of Cindy Hudgins Brizzolara, Houston, TX; *Evening Star* (Washington, D.C.), March 8, 1907; *Times Dispatch* (Richmond, VA), December 8, 1949; *Daily Press* (Newport News, VA), February 1, 1945.

220. Hornberger and Turbyville, *Forgotten Beacons*, 78; *Baltimore Sun*, September 20, 1907; *Light List* (1907), 136; *Daily Press* (Newport News, VA), February 28, 1935; de Gast, *Lighthouses*, 149.

221. *Daily Press* (Newport News, VA), June 14, 1941; *Daily Press* (Newport News, VA), January 6, 1942; *Daily Press* (Newport News, VA), October 15, 1979; *Daily Press* (Newport News, VA), October 22, 1979.

Chapter 11

222. William C. Davis, *Duel Between the First Ironclads* (Garden City, NY: Doubleday, 1975), 76–104; *ORN* 7:4–5; *Official Records of the War of the Rebellion: A Compilation of the Official Records of the United States and Confederate Armies (Washington, D.C., 1881–1901)*, 9: 8–13 (quotation on 9) (Hereinafter *OR*.).

223. John L. Worden, "Report of Captain John L. Worden…*Monitor*, March 9, 1862," *Tyler's Quarterly Historical and Genealogical Magazine* 3, no. 2 (October 1922): 100–6 (quotation on 104); *ORN* 7:4–5; *OR* 9:8–10.

224. John V. Quarstein and Parke S. Rouse Jr., *Newport News: A Centennial History* (Newport News, VA: City of Newport News, 1996), 58–59.

225. George Eldridge, comp., *Eldridge's Coast Pilot No. 2: Southern Section from Chatham to Rio Grande* (Boston, MA: S. Thaxter and Son, 1883), 284; *AR-Treasury* (1890), 94 (quotation); *AR-Treasury* (1888), 81; *Alexandria Gazette*, December 22, 1886; Alan B. Flanders and Arthur C. Johnson Jr., *Guardians of the Capes: A History of Pilots and Piloting in Virginia Waters from 1611 to the Present* (Lively, VA: Brandywine, 1991), 47; James F. Gregory to secretary of the treasury, December 21, 1889, Treasury Department Change Orders (historical documents From the National Archives); Middle Ground Lighthouse, "J.C. Mallery to Chair of the Light-House Board, April 15, 1889, in Letterbook," History, www.middlegroundlight.com/history.

226. *Abridgement of the Nautical Almanac and Tide Tables, 1893, with a List of Lighthouses* (New York: John Bliss, 1892), 37; Middle Ground Lighthouse, "Instruction to Bidders, 9–11," www.middlegroundlight.com/history; Clifford, *Historic Light Stations*, 319.

227. Middle Ground Lighthouse, "J.C. Mallery to Chairman of the Light-House Board, April 22, 1889, Letterbook," www.middlegroundlight.com/history; Middle Ground Lighthouse, "Instruction to Bidders," 9,16 www.middlegroundlight.com/history; Middle Ground Lighthouse, "Descriptive Pamphlet, 5, 13," www.middlegroundlight.com/history.

228. *Light List* (1907), 136; *Daily Press* (Newport News, VA), March 22, 1891; Clifford, *Historic Light Stations*, 319; Middle Ground Lighthouse, "Descriptive Pamphlet, 4–5," www.middlegroundlight.com/history.

229. Middle Ground Lighthouse, "Arthur M. Meekins Field Questionnaire, Sept. 21, 1928, in *Duties of the Lighthouse Keeper*," www.middlegroundlight. com/history.

230. *Richmond Dispatch*, December 9, 1904.

231. *ORP* (1901), 354.

232. Alexander Cosby Brown, ed., *Newport News' 325 Years: A Record of the Progress of a Virginia Community* (Newport News, VA: Newport News Golden Anniversary Committee, 1946), 62, 297, 314–15; Rouse, *Good Old Days*, 73–76.

233. Board of Engineers for Rivers and Harbors, comp., *Ports of Norfolk*, 17; *Daily Press* (Newport News, VA), May 1, 1909; *Evening Star* (Washington, D.C.), August 10, 1903; *Washington Post*, January 18, 1910.

234. *AR-Treasury* (1898), 512; *Evening Star* (Washington, D.C.), August 2, 1910; *Evening Star* (Washington, D.C.), April 7, 1912; *Evening Star* (Washington, D.C.), April 17, 1912; *Evening Star* (Washington, D.C.), August 27, 1915; *ORP* (1909), 305; *CD-Newport News* (1909), 92; *CD-Newport News* (1916), 102.

235. "Ice Damage," *Lighthouse Service Bulletin* 2, no. 2 (February 1, 1918): 9; Middle Ground Lighthouse, "Letterbook, Feb. 3–27, 1918," www. middlegroundlight.com/history.

236. *Official Bulletin* 1, no. 120 (September 29, 1917): 13 (quotation); *AR-Commerce* (1921), 61; *AR-Commerce* (1920), 57.

237. Nancollas, *Seashaken Houses*, 128–29; *Daily Press* (Newport News, VA), December 20, 1937; *Daily Press* (Newport News, VA), July 13, 1938.

238. Department of Commerce, *Wartime Information To Mariners: Supplementing the United States Coast Pilots* (Washington, D.C.: Department of Commerce, 1944), 61.

239. Parke Rouse Jr., *The James: Where a Nation Began* (Richmond, VA: Dietz Press, 1994), 200–1.

240. Find a Grave, "Cleon Curtis 'Sunny' Tillett, memorial no. (125443728) buried at Disciple Church Cem., Manteo, NC," www.findagrave.com; David Wright and David Zoby, *Fire on the Beach: Recovering the Lost Story of Richard Etheridge and the Pea Island Lifesavers* (New York: Simon & Schuster, 2001), passim; *Journal of Newport News Middle Ground Light Station*, "Men attached 6/30/49," www.middlegroundlight.com/history; Middle Ground Lighthouse, "Record of the Miscellaneous Events of the Day [August 1952]," www.middlegroundlight.com/history.

241. *U.S. Navy Hydrographic Office, Radio Navigational Aids* (Washington, D.C.: U.S. Navy Hydrographic Office, 1955), 2–26; Levitt, *Short, Bright Flash*,

231; *Daily Press* (Newport News, VA), May 7, 1947; *Virginian-Pilot* (Norfolk, VA), July 22, 1954; *Virginian-Pilot* (Norfolk, VA), April 16, 1960; *Ledger-Dispatch* (Norfolk, VA), October 23, 1954.

242. *Virginian-Pilot* (Norfolk, VA), July 22, 1954; *Light List* (1970), 344.

243. Turbyville, *Bay Beacons*, 117; *Daily Press* (Newport News, VA), September 24, 2000; *Daily Press* (Newport News, VA), May 12, 2002.

244. *Wall Street Journal*, August 16, 2013; Virginia Department of Historic Resources, "Newport News Middle Ground: National Register of Historic Places Registration," https://www.dhr.virginia.gov/historic-registers/121-0020/; *Virginian-Pilot* (Norfolk), February 7, 2003; *Virginian-Pilot* (Norfolk), July 27, 2005; *Daily Press* (Newport News, VA), August 1, 2005.

245. *Daily Press* (Newport News, VA), March 5, 2006; *Daily Press* (Newport News, VA), July 9, 2006.

246. Nancollas, *Seashaken Houses*, 141.

247. Dolin, *Brilliant Beacons*, 407; *Daily Press* (Newport News, VA), March 5, 2006; Pam Majumdar, "Tripping the Light Fantastic," *Hampton Roads Magazine* (May/June 2008): 59–62; Angela Blue, "Middle Ground Lighthouse," *Coastal Virginia Magazine*, May 27, 2016, www.coastalvirginiamag.com/April-2016/Middle-Ground-Lighthouse/; *Billingsley-Gonsoulin Fact Sheet and Report*, 2023.

INDEX

ABOUT THE AUTHOR

Benjamin H. Trask has more than twenty years of teaching experience, mostly as a middle school history teacher. He holds an undergraduate degree in education and a master of arts degree in history, both from Virginia Tech. Following his time at Virginia Tech, he served as a communications officer in the United States Marine Corps. In 1987, he returned to graduate school, earning a master of science degree in library science from the University of North Carolina–Chapel Hill. Prior to teaching, he was the librarian and a curator at The Mariners' Museum in Newport News. His exhibits, presentations and publications revolve around yellow fever, the American Civil War, maritime affairs and Black American history.

From 2013 to 2021, he worked as a deckhand and narrator aboard *Miss Hampton II*, a harbor cruise boat. From this floating classroom, he shared with visitors the story of the five light stations in the Hampton Roads area. A navy brat and a longtime resident of Hampton, he enjoys writing, exercising, origami and, of course, history road trips.

Visit us at
www.historypress.com